AL-ALAMEIN REVISITED

Proceedings of a Symposium Held on 2 May 1998,
at the American University in Cairo:

The Battle of al-Alamein
and its Historical Implications

Keynote Speaker,
Professor Sir Michael Howard, M.C.

Edited by Jill Edwards

The American University in Cairo

Dar el Kutub No. 17604/99
ISBN 977 424 571 7

Printed in Egypt

AL-ALAMEIN REVISITED

Contents

Contributors

Dr. Frank E. Vandiver Professor Emeritus of Military History, Texas A&M University;
Acting President, the American University in Cairo, 1997–98

Sir Michael Howard, M.C., D. Litt. Chichele Professor of the History of War, 1977, Regius Professor of Modern History, 1980–89, Oxford University;
Robert A. Lovett Chair of Military and Naval History, 1989–93, Yale University

Dr. Raimondo Luraghi Professor Emeritus, University of Genoa; Honorary President of the Italian Society for Military History Italian Representative on the International Committee of Military History

Dr. Peter Liddle Formerly Keeper of the Liddle Collections of the Brotherton Library, University of Leeds;
Currently Director, War Experience Centre: The Second World War, Leeds

Col. (Rtd.) Dr. Ernst-Heinrich Schmidt Director, the Wehrgeschichtliches Museum, Rastatt, 1978–87;
Officer-in-charge of the Military History Museums and Collections of the Federal Armed Forces at the Military History Research Office, Freiburg, 1987–93

Dr. Thomas Scheben Representative of the Konrad Adenauer Foundation for Egypt, 1994–99

Editor:
Dr. Jill Edwards Professor of History, The American University in Cairo

Maps

Editorial Note

The inspiration for this symposium came from Dr. Frank E. Vandiver, then Acting President of the American University in Cairo. The late Sheikh Kamal Adham supported the project with his customary generosity towards the American University in Cairo, and thanks are due also to Vice Provost Dr John Swanson and the team from the President's Office, who coordinated the meeting.

The papers collected here under the title *Al-Alamein Revisited* acknowledge the compelling nature of the history of this famous battlefield that still draws visitors to its desert site and monuments. Those memorials also recall not only the wide variety of military and strategic aspects of the campaigns known collectively as al-Alamein, but reflect different national perspectives characterized in these papers.

As the keynote speaker, Michael Howard sets these battles in their international and historical context. To do this, he returns first to the nineteenth century, to Britain's occupation of Egypt in the 1880s and its rivalry with the fading Ottoman Empire, before giving a masterly overview of the place of al-Alamein in the history of World War II. Mussolini undoubtedly overextended himself with his imperial ambitions in North Africa. But worse, as Raimondo Luraghi's paper demonstrates, the Duce's tragically underequipped forces were committed to North Africa without any reasonable chance of success and with little support since Hitler was trapped in his campaign in the Soviet Union. Some of the survivors of Mussolini's misconceived ambitions, including Professor Luraghi himself, lived to fight for the Allies in the last stages of the war in Europe.

Dr. Thomas Scheben's paper, which he was unable to present at the symposium but which is also included here in an extended version, gives a detailed analysis of the problems facing the German armies in the desert war. His account draws on his excellent multinational bibliography. His detailed chronology of events is also included.

Following a different theme, archivist-historian Peter Liddle uses his unique collection of letters, memoirs, etc. to demonstrate not only the ghastliness of war, but also the clarity with which the ordinary soldier saw his fate and movingly recorded details of daily life in the desert.

In support of and counterpoint to this was the experience of Ernst-Heinrich Schmidt in refurbishing the museum at al-Alamein. His labors there were clearly personal as well as professional. His task is described in terms of creating a living and distinctive memorial for his seven cousins killed in action at or around al-Alamein as much as in representing the hundred thousand more like them, from both sides, whose deaths are symbolized in the artifacts assembled at the al-Alamein Museum.

As Dr. Schmidt's paper makes clear, the idea behind the refurbishment of the museum was that it should advance the cause of peace rather than glorify war. The same idea is reflected in each of the papers gathered here, for rarely have the follies and anguish of war been more clearly underlined than in the history of the battles of al-Alamein.

Foreword

World War II plunged the Middle East into conflict. Axis pressure came initially from Benito Mussolini's ill-conceived notion of extending Italian power across North Africa and consolidating everything from Algeria to Somaliland. Adolf Hitler had to help Mussolini, and did it effectively by sending German troops and a rising new commander, Erwin Rommel, to rescue a failing effort. He arrived in February 1941, and began an amazing series of campaigns back and forth across the North African desert—sometimes winning, sometimes retreating. Always starved of supplies (his operations conflicted with Hitler's Russian commitments), Rommel nonetheless pinned down large British forces. He suggested to Hitler that support of his campaigns might enable him to take the Suez Canal and move into the Caucasus. But by then Hitler's imagination had frozen in Russia.

Prime Minister Winston Churchill, always concerned with North Africa, made one of his bravest decisions late in 1940 when he decided, against all logic, to send some of the few forces available in England to sustain North Africa. He watched operations there, sacked some commanders and, finally, in August 1942, after a personal Cairo visit, brought in a winning team—General Harold Alexander as theater commander, and General Bernard Law Montgomery as commander of the Eighth Army.

Alexander, a brilliant soldier and uncommonly affable man, found an effective way to use his unruly, arrogant, and egotistical subordinate: give him the help he needed and leave him alone. When Alexander and 'Monty' took charge, Rommel had already been halted along the al-Alamein line. Montgomery proceeded to arrange a set-piece battle in which he outnumbered the Germans in both men and tanks (many new ones were on the way from the United States) and attacked on 23 October, 1942. Rommel, on sick leave in Germany, returned in time to lead a retreat that would continue until the final surrender of Axis forces in North Africa.

Al-Alamein ranks as one of the truly decisive battles of World War II. At the end of the campaign Churchill would say that the liberation of North Africa did not mean the beginning of the end of the war, but perhaps the end of the beginning. So important is the battle that it seemed altogether proper that the American University in Cairo—with its constant interest in Egyptian history and international affairs—sponsor a conference on al-Alamein. Scholars from England, Egypt, Germany, Italy, and the United States accepted invitations to share their views on that cataclysmic battle which changed the outcome of the twentieth century's greatest conflict.

These proceedings are the fruits of that enlightening conference.

Frank E. Vandiver

AL-ALAMEIN REVISITED

Map 1:

Rommel's Breakthrough Strategy, late June 1942

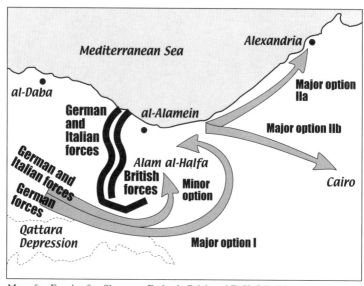

Map after Eppele after Skaruppe, Esebeck, Briel, and E.-H. Schmidt

Michael Howard

The Battle of al-Alamein

The first question that posterity is likely to ask is how and why the Battle of al-Alamein came to be fought at all. What were British, Italian, and German troops, to say nothing of those from as far afield as India, Australia, New Zealand, and South Africa, doing in Egypt and Libya during the first half of the twentieth century?

The British were there first. They had occupied Egypt in the 1880s as part of their imperial expansion in the Middle East in the wake of the disintegrating Ottoman Empire. They moved in mainly to ensure the security of the newly dug Suez Canal, which they saw as their lifeline to their Empire in India and the Far East. The Italians came next, occupying Libya in 1912, also as part of the pickings from a dissolving Ottoman Empire. They hoped to link it up with their imperial acquisitions in East Africa, to which they were to add Abyssinia in 1935. During World War I, the British declared Egypt a 'Protectorate,' effectively making it part of their Empire, to deny it to the Turks and as a useful place d'armes where all their imperial forces could be assembled to complete the conquest of Turkey's Asian possessions and possibly to enter Europe through the back door of the Balkans. After the war, Egyptian nationalist agitation forced the British to promise political independence, which was confirmed by treaty in 1936; but they remained in military occupation, and in the 1930s increased the size of their garrison as Mussolini's Fascist Italy became more threatening. The Egyptians only reluctantly acquiesced. To many in their political classes, including King Farouk himself, it was not clear that Italian occupation would be any worse than British. The British thus found themselves in the anomalous position of defending the territory of an allegedly sovereign power whose primary concern was to see the backs of them.

Then came World War II which Italy entered in June 1940, hoping to extend her empire on the cheap. Three months later, against the advice of his military leaders and without consulting his allies, Mussolini launched a halfhearted and ill-prepared attack on Egypt which fizzled out a few miles beyond the frontier. Hitler himself regarded, and continued to regard, the war in the Mediterranean as a sideshow that distracted forces from his real objective, the attack on the Soviet Union. But for the British it was the only theater where their land forces could be engaged. During the summer of 1940, while German invasion still seemed probable, Churchill took the enormous gamble of sending armored reinforcements that could ill be spared from the defense of Britain itself to reinforce General Wavell's garrison in Egypt. The gamble paid off handsomely. In December Wavell counterattacked into Libya, drove the Italian forces out of the entire Western Desert, and followed up by reconquering the whole of Italian East Africa. The effect on British morale at home and British prestige throughout the world was tremendous. The Mediterranean became the center of British public attention, especially Winston Churchill's attention, and he continued to send there all the forces he could spare.

Against his will, Hitler now had to take account of this shift in strategic focus. Not only did he have to save his ally from total humiliation, but also he knew that the British, from their Middle Eastern base, were trying to put together an alliance with Yugoslavia, Greece, and Turkey that might threaten the southern flank of his forthcoming attack on the Soviet Union. This distant squabble between colonial powers now had to be taken seriously. So in April 1941 he sent a small force, ultimately some three divisions strong, under junior general Erwin Rommel, as what he called a *Sperrverband*—a blocking force—to prevent the British from exploiting their victories in North Africa any further while German forces invaded and cleared up the Balkans. But simultaneously Wavell detached a substantial chunk of his forces from the

Western Desert to help the Greeks repel the invasion of their country. These were caught up in a general rout that ended only with the German conquest of Crete. Meanwhile Rommel, probing British defences in the Western Desert, found little resistance and, in defiance of orders from Berlin, followed up with an attack that drove the British back to the Egyptian frontier. So by the summer of 1941 the colonial war against the Italians had become a front in the war against Germany—and still the only front on which British ground troops were fighting.

Arguably the British should now have cut their losses, stood on the defensive in Egypt, and sent such forces as they could spare to the Far East, where the Japanese were posing a yet greater threat. That, indeed, was the advice given by the Chiefs of Staff. But for Churchill himself, and for British public opinion in general, the whole war now seemed concentrated into a duel with Rommel, whose military skills, considerable though they were, were blown up to heroic proportions by the British press to explain the lamentable performance of their own generals. But there was also a widespread fear that Hitler had ambitious plans for conquering the entire Middle East. This was not, in fact, the case. Indeed, the German High Command were so suspicious of Rommel's own ambitions that they kept him on a very short rein indeed, sending him only minimal reinforcements. Churchill continued to send to the Middle East all the forces he could spare, and by autumn the British forces in Egypt—now designated 'the Eighth Army'— were again ready to take the offensive.

The Eighth Army attacked in November 1941, and there followed eight months of confused campaigning across the Western Desert in which the British came off considerably the worse. By July 1942 Rommel had driven them back deep into Egypt, and they were fighting desperately to hold the last defensible position before Cairo—the forty-mile gap at al-Alamein between the sea in the north and the virtually impassable Qattara Depression to the south. Mussolini flew to Tripoli, complete with white horse, ready to make his triumphal entry into Cairo. In Cairo itself the British were making preparations for general evacuation, and Axis sympathizers were coming out of the woodwork who would welcome Rommel as a liberator. Nor was this all. In south Russia, German forces had reached the Caucasus and were driving south towards the Persian frontier. Whether he planned it or not, Hitler now seemed poised to conquer the entire Middle East in a gigantic pincer movement. At the same time, in the Far East, Japanese armies—having overrun the Malay Peninsula, Singapore and Burma—now stood at the gates of India, while their navy threatened Britain's communications to the Middle East through the Indian Ocean. True, the United States had now entered the war, but American attention was focused on their own disasters in the Pacific. It was a bad moment—perhaps the worst of the entire war.

It is important to realize just how serious the situation seemed at the time if we are to appreciate the complete transformation that was brought about by the battle of al-Alamein three months later. The principal credit for this transformation must go to Winston Churchill, if only for persuading his American allies to take the Mediterranean seriously. For Churchill the Middle East was always the true fulcrum of the war, the only theater where the forces of the British Empire could be united and deployed and through which substantial help could be channelled to their Russian allies. (Oil was important, but not so important as it is today; most of Britain's oil supplies still came across the Atlantic). For most Americans the real war was that being fought in the Pacific. Even those who, like General Marshall, believed in giving priority to the European theater were not enamored of the Mediterranean as a theater of war. For them—as for Hitler—this was a colonial sideshow. They were not fighting to defend the British Empire, any more than Hitler was fighting to extend the Italian. They wanted to accumulate their forces in the British Isles themselves in preparation for a massive attack across the Channel—if possible at once, and certainly no later than 1943.

But during the summer of 1942, in ferociously tough discussions, the British managed to persuade their allies that this simply would not be possible before 1943, and President Roosevelt insisted for political reasons that something had to be done to get American forces engaged in the European theater in 1942. Reluctantly, therefore, the Americans accepted Churchill's 'Mediterranean Strategy.' General Eisenhower at the time dubbed it 'the blackest day in history,' and there are those who still believe that he was right. Simultaneously, with a renewed British offensive in the Western Desert, American and British forces would land in

French North Africa. Between them they would squeeze the Axis forces out of North Africa, clear the Mediterranean (thus releasing great quantities of shipping from the Cape route), and then be in a favorable position to invade Europe itself.

British operations in the Western Desert were now firmly geared to a global strategy, and this time they had to succeed. Everything possible was done to ensure that they would. Substantial numbers of American tanks—Grants and Shermans—were sent to arm the British forces (until the very end of the war the British seemed incapable of manufacturing tanks that could match the Germans), and maximum air cover was provided. Air strength was particularly important, not just over the battlefield itself, but also for cutting the enemy lifeline across the Mediterranean. Rommel was still kept short of supplies by a German High Command who needed everything they could lay hands on for their last desperate thrust towards the oil of the Caucasus, but Allied air attacks kept him still shorter. Allied signal intelligence was able to intercept Rommel's increasingly anxious demands for supplies as he saw the size of the forces building up against him; and here, perhaps, the Allies enjoyed the greatest advantage of all. In the summer of 1942, at the blackest moment of the war, the balance of advantage in radio intelligence swung decisively to the Allied side. The code-breakers at Bletchley achieved a permanent breakthrough into German army ciphers while almost simultaneously Rommel's own sources in Cairo were exposed and destroyed. General Montgomery was to go into battle on 23 October not only with a crushing superiority in armor and air power, but also with a virtually complete knowledge of what was going on 'on the other side of the hill.'

Now for General Montgomery—the key figure in the battle itself. To understand his achievement we need to know something of the British forces of which he took command when he appeared fresh from England on 13 August 1942.

At the beginning of the war the British troops in Egypt—and remember that the term 'British' includes Indian, Australian, New Zealand, and South African—were something of an elite force. The British and Indian troops were professional soldiers, the Dominion troops enthusiastic volunteers. The Italian forces that Wavell had defeated consisted mainly of unhappy conscripts and badly commanded 'native' levies, armed with obsolete equipment. But as the

Eighth Army expanded, it got worse. Officers were promoted above their level of competence, and the ranks filled up with national servicemen with little military skill or experience. In addition, the British Army had no tradition of *la grande guerre*, warfare on a large scale, and such as it had acquired during the First World War had been rapidly forgotten. The peacetime army was trained for small-scale colonial warfare, particularly on the Indian frontier. Its leaders thought in terms of regiments—small introverted families—rather than divisions and corps and armies. Few British officers had commanded more than a brigade, or ever expected to. There was no peacetime training in higher command. In a confrontation with the Germans, the British were thus amateurs, pitted against the best professionals in the world—and it showed.

Montgomery, on the other hand, was a true professional and, as a result, his colleagues—while admiring him—thought him slightly mad. He was one of the very few officers in the British Army who thought about *la grande guerre* and equipped himself to fight it. He had no time for the cozy, clubbable regimental system that made peacetime soldiering in the British Army such a pleasant and gentlemanly lifestyle. He had no intellectual interests. He had very few friends. He engaged in no field sports. He thought only about war, and he thought about it with rigorous and sustained clarity. He had trained himself for high command, there being no one else to train him. So when the necessary tools were put into his hands, he knew how to use them.

Further, unlike most of his colleagues, he understood the importance of publicity. Most British generals hated and mistrusted the press. Montgomery not only courted personal publicity but also understood how important it was in enabling him to communicate with his troops and raise their morale. He rapidly adopted a style of dress to distinguish himself from all the other British generals, and used his press contacts to persuade the world and his own men that they were a force quite distinct from the rest of the British Army—a *corps d'elite* in which it was an honor to serve. He was understandably regarded by most of the old hands in the Western Desert as a perfectly intolerable little man, and many of them continued to dislike him even at the height of his success.

Montgomery had one further advantage denied to his unfortunate predecessor, General Auchinleck. Auchinleck, like Wavell, had commanded the whole of the Middle East, but the incompetence of his subordinate commanders had forced him to take personal command of the fighting in the Western Desert. He did so at a moment when the German advance in the Caucasus was threatening not only his own rear but also the very frontiers of India, where Auchinleck had spent his entire military career. So at the most critical moment of the fighting in the Western Desert, Auchinleck was looking over his shoulder to see what was happening in Persia and Iraq, and he would have been more than human if he had not been distracted. Montgomery had none of those worries. Auchinleck had been replaced as GOC (general officer commanding) Middle East by General Sir Harold Alexander, a general who had his own kind of charisma but who recognized Montgomery's exceptional qualities and left him alone to get on with his job. Montgomery's admirers have been less than fair to Auchinleck. He had, after all, won what can be called the First Battle of al-Alamein, in July, which had checked Rommel's advance on Cairo and stabilized the front line. None the less Montgomery, on his arrival from England, found his forces, as Churchill put it, 'brave but baffled'—some of them outright defeatist, none of them with any idea what to do next.

The matter was taken out of their hands two weeks later when, on 31 August, Rommel launched a new attack in what is now known as the Battle of Alam al-Halfa. Thanks to his intelligence sources, Montgomery was ready for him. He established his forces in strong positions from which he refused to be lured, and smashed Rommel's panzer formations by a combination of artillery and close-support air power. This not only destroyed Rommel's last chance of taking Cairo; it also established Montgomery's reputation as a man capable of living up to his own claims, and when he himself took the offensive the following October it was with an army that had a confidence in his professional competence that had been forfeited by his predecessors.

I won't go into the details of the battle. Fought as it was on a narrow front without any possibility of outflanking, it resembled rather a battle of attrition from the First World War than anything seen in the Second, and Montgomery was able to use all the skills that he had acquired during that war as a staff officer on the Western Front. He had a two-fold superiority in every arm: nearly

200,000 men to the Axis' 100,000, of which only half were German; over 1,000 tanks to the enemy's 500, of which only 200 were German; and 2,300 guns to the enemy's 1,200, of which—again—only half were German. Only in aircraft did Rommel's forces enjoy something like equality, and those were crippled by lack of fuel. But Rommel had deployed his forces skillfully in depth behind well-sited minefields, and kept his best forces back for counterattack. Montgomery did not rely on numbers alone. His logistical preparations were almost faultless, and he used deception skillfully to conceal both the timing of the attack (which came when Rommel was on leave in Germany) and the direction of his main thrust. But above all, again like a general of the First World War, he was prepared where necessary to accept heavy losses. In the twelve days of hard fighting that the battle lasted, from 23 October to 4 November, the Eighth Army lost 13,500 men, about eight percent of the forces engaged. But Rommel lost at least 8,000 in killed and wounded and 30,000 taken prisoner, most of them because there was no fuel to enable them to get away. He abandoned 1,000 guns and 450 tanks on the battlefield. His forces were shattered, and he was unable to make a serious stand until he reached Tunisia, four months later and 1,500 miles further west.

Montgomery has been blamed for not exploiting the mobility of his armored forces and preventing Rommel from escaping altogether. There is something in this; but the management of an army 200,000 strong on the move is tricky even for experienced professionals, and Montgomery still did not entirely trust the capacity of some of his divisional and corps commanders. Rommel's escape was to make the final roundup of Axis forces in Tunisia the following spring a more difficult business, but there were many other reasons why the Allies took six months to clear the coast of North Africa. What mattered was the victory at al-Alamein and the scale of it. Arguably it was the greatest British victory since Waterloo, and at home it was treated as such. Church bells rang out (they had been silenced since the summer of 1940 when they would be used to give warning of an invasion), services of thanksgiving were held, and the British people—with some reason—began to think themselves great again. "Before Alamein," Churchill was to write with some exaggeration, "we had never had a victory. After it we never had a defeat."

Churchill also termed the battle "the turning point in the Hinge of Fate." This was not untrue, but it was a very insular perspective. It would be more accurate to say that the real turning point came a week later on the night of 7 November, when American forces landed on the shores of French North Africa, ensuring the commitment of the vast strength of their nation to victory in Europe. But a yet more significant event came twelve days later on 19 November, when the Russians opened the counterattacks that were to trap the German Sixth Army in Stalingrad and inflict on the Wehrmacht its first, gigantic, and irrevocable defeat. But perhaps the true significance of al-Alamein and the successful pursuit that followed it, was to ensure that Britain remain in the war on a basis of equality with her stronger allies. It restored her self-respect and the respect in which she was held by others—not least in the United States—and it prolonged for another decade her hegemonical position in the Middle East. We have only to consider what the situation would have been in Cairo if Montgomery had lost the battle to appreciate the full significance of his victory.

Further, it was to be the last all-British victory in the European theater of war. Perhaps Churchill's own 'finest hour' came in Tripoli in February 1943, when he reviewed a march-past of the Eighth Army, the last combined forces of the British Empire—bronzed, triumphant young men from Britain, South Africa and the Antipodes, to say nothing of those of the Indian Army still unswervingly loyal to the Raj. All campaigns thereafter had to be fought in association with an increasingly powerful and demanding American ally. Indeed one reason, and to my mind not the least important, why Churchill fought so stubbornly throughout the last years for the continuation of the war in the Mediterranean, rather than transferring the main allied thrust to northwest Europe as the Americans wanted, was that it was in that theater that the British still enjoyed a preponderance of forces and British generals held the senior commands. He was determined that the hard-won laurels of victory should not be snatched away from the brows of those who had done so much to deserve them.

But perhaps to posterity all these considerations will seem very parochial, and the lasting significance of the battle will be this: it was the last time that European powers conducted their wars on non-European territory and largely over the heads of its inhabitants. The era that had opened in the sixteenth century during which Spanish, Portuguese, Dutch, French, English, Italians, and Germans had competed for empire all over the world; when English and Dutch had fought one another in the East Indies and Dutch and Spaniards in the West, French and British in North America and India, and British and Germans in South Africa—this had all come to an end. A decade later the British would recognize political realities and leave Egypt for good. British military power had been effective in repelling other European armies, but it could not indefinitely suppress the determination of the Egyptian people to achieve the freedoms for which, allegedly, the Second World War had been fought. But al-Alamein meant that the British Empire went out with a bang rather than a whimper.

Raimondo Luraghi

The Italian Forces at the Battle of al-Alamein
*'Ferrea Mole, Ferreo Cuore'**

There is a tendency in British and German historiography of the Second World War to belittle the Italian contribution to military operations, if not to ignore it altogether. This is largely because few historians read Italian or consult Italian military sources. Moreover, residual Italo-phobic sentiment, subconsciously perhaps, remains an obstacle to reaching balanced, unbiased assessments. According to one American historian, "not a few ... would like to trade their place in the carpool seat for a seat in a Spitfire during the battle of Britain. It is a safe bet, though, that only a peculiar few nurse the desire to pilot an MC 202 or join the Ariete Division, since for most readers of English, the former could be a brand of pasta and the latter a rock group." He continues, "Of course, most Italians could easily identify the Macchi as a high-performance fighter aircraft and the Ariete as a crack Italian armored unit."[1] Unfortunately, the prejudice of the former group tends to be the more prevalent. Even the most serious of British and German historians tend to consider the Battle of al-Alamein— which, between 23 October and 5 November 1942, decided the war in the Western Desert—as some kind of Anglo–German 'private affair,' ignoring the contribution and, indeed, even the presence of the Italians. Actually, it is incorrect to speak only of British

---

* 'Iron Skin, Iron Heart'— the motto of the Italian tank crews.

troops, since on the Allied side there were Australians, New Zealanders, South Africans, Indians, French, Greeks, and even American aviators.

In fact, as Field Marshal Montgomery's buildup for his great offensive neared completion, the proportion of Italian to German forces was as shown in Table 1.[2]

TABLE 1:
RELATIVE STRENGTHS OF ITALIAN AND GERMAN FORCES

	Italians	Germans	Total
Men	54,000	50,000	104,000
Infantry Battalions	41	28	69
Field guns	371	200	571
Antitank guns	150	372	522
Antiaircraft guns	740	600	1,340
Armored cars	72	47	119
Tanks	279	211	490
Aircraft	230	110	340

So not only was the Italian contribution to the coming battle consistent, but it was also numerically superior to the German, and these statistics should be taken into account. True, the Italians needed German help in North Africa. But why was this, and what was the German contribution to the war economy of the African front? The Italian soldiers sent to North Africa, despite denigrating propaganda, were—in the main—good fighters; this was acknowledged by unbiased German and British witnesses.[3] Why, then, were they defeated by the British in 1940?

The weakest point in the Italian army was its lack of firepower. Comparison between the Italian and British infantry divisions suffices to explain this: see Table 2.[4] The figures speak for themselves. The Italian division's firepower was almost negligible in comparison with that of the British and Commonwealth. Yet the greatest weakness of the Italian units lay in their field transportation. While the British division and its components were motorized, the Italians moved on foot just as in World War I. This was absurd in desert warfare, where mobility was indispensable for any military operation. It was this that made it possible for the numerically inferior, yet overwhelmingly better equipped, British army to defeat the bigger, but poorly armed, Italian army.

	Italian	British and Commonwealth
Men	7,000	17,300
Machine guns	238	1,263
Heavy mortars	18	56
Light mortars	—	162
[Total mortars	18	218]
Field guns	60	72
Antitank guns	72	136
Vehicles	214	2,267
Light armor	—	256
Armored cars	—	6

The explanation for this discrepancy lies in factors predating the campaign itself and essential to understanding how the Italians came to give so good an account of themselves at al-Alamein. According to one authoritative source, "immediately before the war, Italian infantry strength was equal to that of the major armies. Unfortunately, while elsewhere studies and improvements went on steadily in order to keep up with the most advanced military teachings of the war, we remained at the same level."[5]

This caused serious backwardness in field armament, since the Italian General Staff remained convinced that Italy would fight a mountain war where it was assumed only light three-ton tanks would be of use.[6] For the same reason, but also from a kind of mental inertia, the Italian Staff never seriously tackled the problem of motorized transport.[7]

Yet the fault should not be placed exclusively on the Italian military.[8] During the four years following 1935, Italy was involved in continuous war: first the Ethiopian war, then the Spanish Civil War. Germany sent Spain a limited number of highly specialized forces for limited periods. Italy, on the other hand, sent and kept in Spain an expeditionary corps (Corpo Truppe Volontarie) of more than 100,000 men who proved decisive to Franco's victory. However, in helping the Nationalist army to its victory, Mussolini robbed Italy's own arsenals. Table 3 is a summary of equipment sent to Spain:

TABLE 3: MILITARY SUPPLIES SENT BY ITALY TO SPAIN DURING THE CIVIL WAR[9]

Army

Cannons	1,801
Mortars	1,426
Machine guns	3,436
Rifles	223,784
Cartridges	320,000,000
Explosives (tons)	2,000
Vehicles	7,494
Tanks & armored cars	157

Navy

Ships and submarines	10
Artillery shells	47,643
Cartridges	115,600
Oil (tons)	5,100

Air Force

Military aircraft	762
Warplane bombs	716,961

To send such enormous amounts of equipment and weaponry, the Italian government foolishly depleted not only its arsenals, but also the resources stockpiled for war emergency, even the reserves of the existing infantry divisions and the newly created Armored Division.[10]

In the end, the real blow—which almost knocked Italy out—was the appalling financial cost of Italian participation in the Spanish Civil War. The Italian Treasury spent 6,086,003,680 Italian lire or, in today's currencies, L7,084,968,284,320 or $3,936,093,491.[11]

Lack of resources explains far more cogently the plight of the Italian army than the supposed backwardness of the General Staff. Soldiers may be brave, but without weapons none can fight, let alone win. This raises the question as to why Mussolini entered the war with the armed forces and the entire country in such lamentable condition. The fact is that, as Renzo De Felice has pointed out, Mussolini was persuaded that Hitler would land in England before long and that the war was almost over.[12]

Still, shortly after receiving their first and vital allocation of German aid (actually just one panzer division), the Italians set to work to repair the situation. They did not lack for will, energy, or ingenuity, but it was an uphill struggle against heavy odds. Not only was the Italian army's power plant inferior to both the German and British, but also the operation of her navy and her limited industrial production were all hampered by shortages of raw materials, mainly oil and coal.[13]

As a result of Herculean effort, the almost useless three-ton tank was replaced in 1941 by the new fourteen-ton M13, armed with a 47 mm gun in a turret. A year later the self-propelled gun with a 75 mm gun in a casemate was added. By late 1940 it was also possible to send to North Africa supplies of the new armored car Mod. 40, with 20 mm gun.

However, no matter how hard Italy tried, because the Allied armies were also upgrading, the task of catching up was near impossible. The new M13 was already almost obsolete when it entered service, yet this was what Italian tank commanders had to make do with in facing British Crusaders, Valentines, and Matildas. They had to resort to putting sandbags over their tanks in the hope of increasing their protection. Eventually, sheer determination made it possible for Italy to send her own armored divisions to North Africa—first the Ariete, which commanded respect of friend and foe alike and later, in 1942, the Littorio and the mechanized division, Trieste.

Of course the German presence, though numerically inferior to the Italian, gave indispensable support during this period while Italy struggled to get its new armor into the lines. Indeed, they supplied the firepower essential to supporting the Italians, who faced the British with ever fewer and inferior arms. While this meant that the Italians were eventually able to die gamely and even inflict substantial blows on the enemy, the formation of one, then two armored divisions and one motorized one had not solved the need for mass motorization. The Italian General Staff and Marshal Badoglio himself in 1939 said that war in North Africa was not possible except with fully motorized troops.[14] By the autumn of 1940 Field Marshal Badoglio was gone from the scene, however, and it seems no one else understood that in desert war the means are more important than the men.[15]

What most hindered the task of motorization was the problem of fuel. Every gallon of oil had to be transported across the Mediterranean where the Royal Navy maintained marked superiority over the Italian Regia Marina. In this the British were aided by their code-breaking knowledge of 'Ultra,' thus knowing in advance the routes and schedules of the Italian convoys. Even after the Italians changed the code, the British followed their movements from decoded German signals. That the British did not entirely succeed in intercepting traffic between Italy and North Africa is a testimony to the courage and determination of the Regia Marina, which won the respect of the Royal Navy, though the latter has been reluctant to acknowledge it.[16]

The real problem, then, was one of supply. Not only every drop of fuel, but also drinking water, ammunition, food, and other supplies had to cover a distance of around 1,300 miles to al-Alamein. This meant that transportation trucks consumed roughly 20 percent of available fuel. British aerial attacks, vehicle breakdown, and other problems accounted for a further diminution of supplies.[17]

And yet fuel was indispensable to meet the challenge from the Royal Air Force, though even here the Italians made progress. The old-fashioned CR42 fighter biplanes were either scrapped or transformed into ground attack planes, and in their place was the new MC 202, a first-rate fighter, as good as the German Messerschmidt 109 and capable of meeting, on equal terms, the British Hurricanes and Spitfires. Since there was no time to retool Italian industry, nor to invent and produce adequate power plant for the new fighter, the problem was solved by buying from Germany the license for the Daimler-Benz DB 601 linear engine.[18] This enabled the Regia Aeronautica to do its fair share of fighting.

TABLE 4: ITALIAN AND GERMAN AIRCRAFT IN GOOD BATTLE ORDER AT THE TIME OF AL-ALAMEIN[19]

	R. Aeronautica	Luftwaffe
Fighters	70	80
Bombers	150	7020
Ground attack, etc.	360	—

By autumn of 1942, however, Italy fielded 1,340 warplanes and Germany 661 in the Mediterranean theater as a whole. It was essential to resume the aerial offensive against Malta. It had been a serious mistake to give up the attacks on the British base in favor of the advance to al-Alamein,[21] one it was now vital to redeem by means of an all-out air offensive. This would have to last two to three weeks, keeping the island under heavy attack, and so allowing Italian convoys carrying supplies for stockpiling to reach ports east of Benghazi. The Regia Marina insisted that this was the only way to solve the problem of supplying the army in North Africa.[22] Yet Hitler refused to reinforce the Luftwaffe in the Mediterranean; all he was prepared to do was to send a group of fighters, and that only after the fall of Stalingrad.[23]

Then on 20 October 1942 Field Marshal Kesselring was forced to halt the air offensive against Malta; the Luftwaffe had lost thirty-eight planes, the Regia Aeronautica ten, against only thirty-two by the Royal Air Force. The loss on 17 October of two Luftwaffe aces was a significant blow. Meanwhile, as a result of the sinking of freighters between 8 and 23 October 1942, the loss of supplies shipped to Libya skyrocketed to 44 percent, those of fuel to 51 percent.[24]

So the prelude to al-Alamein was essentially fought out between Axis and Allied air forces in which the extreme disproportion of combat planes in favor of the Allies accounts for the latter's success. Seven hundred Italian and German war planes were pitted against 1,585 on the Allied side.[25] Of these, 846 were fighters, 716 bombers, and 23 were four-engined flying fortresses.

Enemy bombardment of North Africa began on 9 October 1942, targeting the Axis airstrips at Fuka and Abu Aggag. The enemy inflicted serious damage, forcing Axis fighters to remain airborne in almost continuous combat. For example, on 20 October, Italian fighters took part in eight engagements with enemy bomber squadrons. This was followed the next day with four more defensive sorties in which the Italian air force was outnumbered four to one. Stepping up its offensive, the Allies were able to deploy up to seven hundred war planes a day. Between 22 and 31 October, the Regia Aeronautica lost fifteen MC 202s in combat, with ten more fighters and bombers destroyed on the ground and fifty-four suffering some damage. And this is not counting German losses.[26]

Given the overwhelming superiority of the British in the air, Rommel doubted the Axis army on the ground would be strong enough to sustain an enemy offensive, but refused to consider retreating to safer positions even in order to cut their distance from supplies.[27]

After failing at Alam al-Halfa between 30 August and 5 September, there seemed no reason for the Italian–German army to remain at al-Alamein. Indeed the disproportion between the Axis and Allied armies was already insurmountable, as Table 5 shows.[28]

TABLE 5: FORCES AT AL-ALAMEIN, MID-OCTOBER 1942

	Italians	Germans	Total Axis	British & Allied
Men	54,000	50,000	104,000	195,000
Tanks [light]	279	211	490	1,300
Tanks [heavy]		50	50	300
Armored cars	72	47	119	435
Field guns	371	200	571	908
Antitank guns	150	372	522	1,451
Antiaircraft guns	740	600	1,340	812
Aircraft	230	110	340	973

What made it almost impossible for the Axis to face the Allied enemy was the arrival of the American-built 28.5-ton Grant and 35-ton Sherman tanks with their 75 mm guns in turrets. Equally formidable was the 105 mm Priest SP gun that could reduce an Italian tank to pieces. German tanks could not compete, with the exception of a few Pzkw and 4 Specials which, being lighter, could take on the Grants and Shermans on inferior ground. Italian M13s could do nothing, as shells from their 47 mm guns simply bounced off the armor of such giant tanks like so many cobblestones. Only the Italian self-propelled 75 mm gun—with which the Ariete and Littorio divisions were well supplied—had any hope of success against such heavy enemy tanks. Besides this overwhelming preponderance of superior weaponry, Allied supply bases were only seventy miles away from their lines, compared with the 1,300 miles separating the Axis armies from their own vital supplies.

Furthermore, remaining at al-Alamein meant abandoning the military maneuver employed successfully by Rommel in the past and which he regarded as his trump; this was to lure the enemy into mobile warfare of which he was the master exponent. His best option might have been to increase the gap in front of the British as he retreated to the Sollum-Halfaya line, deploying his mobile forces on his front, not at the rear, as at al-Alamein. By staying at al-Alamein he was forced to stake everything on a passive defense strategy, relying entirely on Axis minefields and firepower. The problem, as he well knew, was that compared with the tremendous firepower of the German infantry, the Italian divisions were weak.[29]

This was the situation, then, in which the Field Marshal took his much-debated decision to dispose his forces in what was called a 'comb line,' interspersing Italian and German troops along the front line. In doing so he hoped the Italians would benefit from superior German firepower, particularly from their antitank guns. They would also profit from access to German radio communications,[30] since their lack of mobility arose partly from poor radio equipment.[31]

It was a rational enough decision. It was taken with the intention of utilizing the fighting spirit of the Italians by supplying them with the fire support they lacked. And yet, by doing so, the Italian battalions lacked proper guidance from their commanding officers, since the Germans frequently forgot to tell their Italian partners of their decisions and commands.

It soon became clear that the decision to engage battle on a static defense line would in itself defeat the Italian infantry divisions. On foot and with no way of retreating, they were forced to fight and die as they stood. Soldiers of both armies understood this and it contributed to their demoralization. Many of the regiments had been in the front line for nearly three years. Their meagre rations of fuel and ammunition had to take priority. This meant that mail from home, food, and water reached them late if at all. Medical supplies failed to arrive, making it almost impossible to tend the wounded and sick, many of whom had dysentery. And yet each soldier knew that the only way to avoid the enemy prison camps and return home was to fight to win. This alone gave them the courage to battle on.[32]

The 'comb' system covered only the northern section of the front, where battalions of the Italian Trento and Bologna divisions were mixed with the German 164th Infantry Division. Next came the Brescia Division, combined with some forces from the Ramcke

Map 2: Italian and German Troops, North Africa 1941

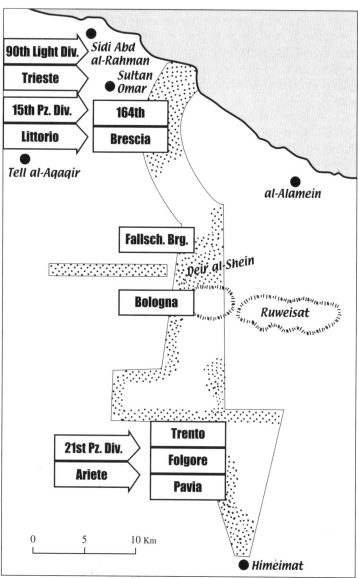

Based on Rommel, *Krieg ohne Hass*; and Gause, *Feldzug in Nordafrika*. Courtesy of E.-H. Schmidt.

Paratroops Brigade. The southern section, down to the impassable Quattara Depression, was almost completely held by Italian units—the crack Folgore Division of paratroops and the Pavia Infantry Division, together with scattered German forces. But the Folgore, an airborne division, had no ground transportation or heavy weapons such as field guns. In the coming battle, however, the paratroops gave excellent support with their few mortars and machine guns, and some field guns from the Pavia Division were used.[33]

This line was purely defensive with an extensive minefield in front. Behind the minefield was an advance line, generally kept by a company from any battalion, then the main defense line two to three miles deep for the last resistance. The main line was composed of a series of isolated strongholds, each defended by a battalion plus field and antitank guns with alternating Italian and German troops. Immediately behind the line the mobile forces were divided into three groups. The Italian motorized Trieste Division was with the German 90th Light Division near the coast; the 15th Panzer Division and the Italian armored Littorio Division were in the north-central zone; the 21st Panzer Division and the Italian armored Ariete Division were in the south-central sector. Such scattered distribution of forces indicates that Rommel had already given up the idea of keeping a powerful concentration of armor to attack the enemy in a mobile battle.

Initially Rommel had intended to keep the mobile forces far back of the main line, ready to give battle if or when the enemy should succeed in breaking through. He soon realized that, in fact, he had no reserves at all. This forced him to take the disastrous decision to use the mobile force as a reserve to plug any gaps the enemy might make in the main defense line,[34] thus destroying virtually all hope of attacking the British army en masse. The Axis mobile forces were to be sent in piecemeal which, in the end, could only result in defeat.

The fateful encounter was about to begin. The day of 23 October drifted slowly by. The British and Allied forces had been ready for several hours. Then, to quote a participant,

at exactly 8:45 p.m. ... the immense desert became overcast by a storm of shells of all sizes raining down over paths, dugouts, observatories and

increasingly onto the advance lines. In the meantime, the sky over our
heads was filled with a deafening roar accompanying the first sight of the
flying fortresses, which we saw in their hundreds through the flashing of
countless rockets which illuminated the sky, changing night to day. Then
the din became so intense that we could no longer tell shell bursts from
aerial bombs or from the sound of enemy gunfire. The entire desert hori-
zon before us was ablaze....[35]

So short of shells were the Axis forces that General Georg
Stumme was obliged to hold fire.[36] Then suddenly, on the morning
of 25 October, Stumme died of a stroke, adding to the confusion in
the Italian–German army. Fortunately, Rommel returned and
quickly resumed command. The enemy attack of the first day was
ferocious, obliterating the defense line and penetrating the main
line. Fighting together, Italians of the 3rd Battalion of the 62nd
Italian Regiment and the German 2nd Battalion of the 382nd
Regiment counterattacked, re-establishing their positions.[37]
Meanwhile the Italian ground attack aircraft, protected by MC
202s and German MS 109s, attacked the enemy lines only to be
repulsed by the magnitude of the RAF operation, which cost them
four Italian planes.[38]

Meanwhile the British 13th Corps, supported by the 7th
Division, unleashed another attack against the southern wing of the
Axis front, while General Koenig's French Brigade tried to out-
flank the Italian position. The intention was plain: immobilized by
the tremendous pressure in the north, the main body of the Axis
forces would not be able to support their outer flank. The British
would break through, advancing in a sweeping line onto the central and northern positions.

However, on the southern flank, paratroops of the Folgore
Division stood firm against formidable odds and, after a ferocious
and particularly bloody battle, repelled the attack. At the very tip
of the southern flank, Lt. Col. Izzo, who was badly wounded in this
action, fought off the entire French Foreign Legion with his single
battalion of the Folgore.[39]

Already in the north, at dawn on 24 October, tanks of the Littorio
armored division together with some of the 15th Panzers had been
sent in and had succeeded in stopping the gap. This was the first
use of these piecemeal mobile forces. After that, however, the two

armored divisions were unable to disentangle themselves from the confusion of the battle. In the early afternoon, after being held temporarily by the point-blank fire of the Trento Division artillery, the enemy reached the field guns and the Littorio went in again. The entire battle was fought at close quarters, and once again the Axis stopped the gap, but at great cost. Because the 47 mm guns of the Italian M13 tanks were almost powerless against the heavily armored British tanks, the Italians had to use their self-propelled 75 mm guns manned by the tank crews. The Littorio lost thirty of its eighty tanks, or almost 38 percent. The British lost forty-one tanks out of 162, or 25 percent. Such losses clearly could not be sustained for long.[40] And yet that night Rommel ordered the Italian artillery of the 22nd Corps and the Deutsche Afrika Korps (DAK), to carry out heavy bombardment of the positions taken by the enemy while the scanty Axis air forces attacked. They struck and set ablaze twenty-five enemy trucks full of supplies and fuel, forcing the enemy onto the offensive.

On the southern wing and ready to attack was General Frattini, commanding the Folgore Division, supported only by a handful of tanks of the Ariete and some German antitank guns. The enemy attacked first, but was beaten back with the loss of thirty-one tanks. In total, during the first days of battle, the British and Allied forces had lost 245 tanks out of 734 engaged. Of their 426 tanks, the Axis had lost 101. Ignoring the protests of the Italians, General von Thoma, commanding the DAK, persisted in sending in his tanks in small isolated groups, thus sustaining serious losses to no avail.[41]

On his return, Rommel had found the Trento Division reduced by seventy percent and facing three enemy infantry divisions and two armored divisions with only two battalions of the 164th Division. But there was no alternative other than to attack with the tattered remains of his army. Meanwhile, despite continued pressure, the Folgore Division held out. But now the systematic deployment of tank formations to stop gaps in the lines was wearing them out.

If he were to continue at all, Rommel knew it must be in a last all-out effort. He therefore decided on a major counterattack. The two remaining armored divisions, the remnants of the Ariete and the 21st Panzer, were recalled from the southern front; the Trieste and the 90th German Light Division were also put into line.

However, the preliminary action by Stuka dive bombers, which should have opened the way for the tanks, failed to do so, as they were swept away by British and American fighters. By early morning on 27 October, despite heavy losses, the 11th Battalion of the 7th Bersaglieri Regiment had taken part of Hill 28, held till then by the Australians. Then the main armor went in, the enemy answering with tremendous artillery fire, attacking at the same time with ninety heavy bombers and bringing the offensive to an immediate halt.

On 2 November, Field Marshal Montgomery began operation 'Supercharge.' The Littorio Division sent in anything it had left: twenty tanks against forty 'Valentines.' This savage struggle was to be the last for the gallant Littorio. At this point, General von Thoma threw in both the German panzer divisions—or at any rate what remained—together with the 11th Tank Brigade of the Trieste Division. Against the firepower of the huge Grant and Sherman tanks with their 75 mm guns, the Italian and German tanks had no choice but to fight on bravely until they were smashed to pieces, losing seventy Germans tanks and fifty Italian.

That same evening, Field Marshal Rommel acknowledged defeat. Now the retreat began, though still resisting. It was started by the southern wing, which was the furthest away. Before dawn on 3 November, the Folgore, Pavia, and Bologna infantry divisions—i.e., the Italian 10th Corps—were able to disengage in good order untroubled by the enemy, due to their own valiant and successful defense against overwhelmingly greater forces.

This orderly retreat might have saved part of the Italian 10th Corps, already decimated though they were by the heavy losses of the preceding days. But on the same day Mussolini and Hitler sent peremptory orders not to retreat. They were to return to their previous position and fight to the end.[42] This sounded the death knell for the Italian 10th Corps. When at last the two dictators grudgingly consented to authorize the retreat "on a new line," it was too late. The British armored and motorized divisions were already ahead of the Italian infantry, closing off any way of escape.

This is how one Folgore veteran assessed it:

> How much better it would have been, then, to remain in the old line, well
> entrenched and with ammunition, food and water which, without trans-

portation, we were obliged to abandon … the Folgore, Brescia, and Pavia were under tremendous and constant fire from the enemy as they made their painful way on foot through the desert, tormented by hunger and thirst [43] In the end they, and even the undefeated Folgore, had to give up. "We don't surrender," said one Italian officer to his English counterpart, "we only stop fighting because we have run out of ammunition."[44]

Such defiant courage from these ragged, thirsty, half-starved, and barefoot men could not but command the respect of their captors.

With the battle of al-Alamein over the only task remaining for Rommel was to retreat across the Libyan border with as many of his forces as possible. But it was almost all over for the last Italian armored division, the Ariete. The enemy's 30th Corps was advancing on a wide arc, keeping the remnants of the DAK under heavy pressure. At the same time, the 7th Armored Division was threatening to flank the few remaining German tanks to their right. In order to intercept them, Rommel had no choice but to deploy his relatively intact Ariete.[45]

The Ariete tank crews understood only too well what their chances against the Grants and Shermans were, but gallantly engaged with them in nearby Deir al-Murra to the right of the 15th Panzer—or what was left of it. They were supported by just one artillery regiment of the Trieste Division, together with the remains of the Littorio. The big enemy tanks stopped out of range and began firing. The Ariete had only the Trieste field pieces that still could not move. Despite this, the Italian tanks closed in daringly. Some enemy tanks were destroyed by fire from the Ariete's 75 mm SP guns. The small M13s fought on valiantly at close quarters but were decimated by the enemy's fire.

Field Marshal Rommel's epicedium to their courage is contained in his account of their action:

> Enormous dust clouds could be seen south and southeast of headquarters, where the desperate struggle of the small and inefficient Italian tanks … was being played out against the hundred or so British heavy tanks. I was told by Major von Luck, whose battalion I had sent to close the gap between the Italians and the Afrika Korps, that the Italians, who at that time represented our strongest motorised force, fought with exemplary courage. Von Luck gave what assistance he could with his guns but was

unable to avert the fate of the Italian Armored Corps. Tank after tank burst or went ablaze, while all the time a tremendous British barrage lay over the Italian infantry and artillery positions.

The last message from the Ariete came at about 1530 hours: "Enemy tanks penetrated south of the Ariete, now surrounded. Location 5 km northwest Bir al-Abd. Ariete's tanks still fighting."

By evening the 20th Italian Corps, though defending gallantly, had been completely destroyed. In the Ariete we lost our oldest Italian comrades, from whom we had probably always demanded more than they, with their poor armament, had been capable of performing.[46]

This was the end of the Ariete, the gallant Italian armored division which, always against heavy odds, had fought valiantly at al-Agheila, Benghazi, Sidi Rezegh, Tobruk, Sollum, Halfaya, Alam al-Halfa, to al-Alamein. One by one its tanks were destroyed. No more than a dozen were able to break through the ring and join the retreating column.

Unfortunately for the poor remnants of the brave Italian forces such as the Folgore, Brescia, and Pavia, a fate worse than defeat or prison camp was reserved. Their worst postwar suffering lay in the slander they suffered from friend and foe alike. It was just too easy to blame defeat on this exhausted group of men. Still worse, they were held accountable for the infamous aggression of the fascist government that had plunged Italy into a war they did not want, nor fully understand. For them it had been a simple matter of duty and patriotism.

For many years academic historians remained blind to the real truth, preferring the easy option of repeating old lies. Only historians such as the late John J. T. Sweet, who were able to read and study Italian documents, were able to reconstruct the truth and present a very different account.

A major American historian studying the dramatic story of the Italian army concluded:

"Unfortunately, in modern war intellectual mastery … meant nothing without technological support. And here, national policy, industrial development, and society had let the (Italian) army down. The *carristi*,[47] despite their motto *'Ferrea Mole, Ferreo Cuore,'* had no iron skin to go with their iron hearts."[48]

NOTES

[1] James J. Sadkovich, "Understanding Defeat: Re-appraising Italy's Role in World War II," *Journal of Contemporary History*, vol. 24, 1989, p. 27ff.

[2] These are the most accurate statistics. See Mario Montanari, *Le Operazioni in Africa Settentrionale, vol. 3, El Alamein,* (Gennaio–Novembre, 1942), Rome, Stato Maggiore Esercito, Ufficio Storico, 1989, p. 705 ff; J. J. Sadkovich, "Understanding Defeat," gives slightly different data, attributing to the Italians forty-two infantry battalions, 259 tanks, and only thirty armored vehicles.

[3] *The Rommel Papers*, ed. B.H. Liddell Hart, New York, 1953, pp. 147 and 373; Correlli Barnett, *The Desert Generals*, London, 1960, p. 37.

[4] Montanari, *Le Operazioni*, p. 742ff.

[5] *L'Esercito Italiano alla Vigilia della Seconda Guerra Mondiale*, Rome, Ufficio Storico dello Stato Maggiore Esercito, 1982, p. 235.

[6] Against France, or even Germany? This question needs serious historical study. See, for a political perspective, the outstanding Renzo De Felice, "Mussolini, il Duce," vol. 3, part 2, *Lo Stato Totalitario, 1936–1940*, Turin, 1981, also an indispensable study for the politics of fascist Italy.

[7] *L'Esercito Italiano alla Vigilia*, p. 236.

[8] The most reliable study of Italian military equipment is by John Joseph Timothy Sweet, *Iron Arm: The Mechanization of Mussolini's Army, 1920–1940*, Greenwood, Connecticut, 1980. He points out that Italian military thought was more advanced than that of many other great powers, and suggests the blame lay rather with politicians, industrialists, and society as a whole.

[9] A. Rovighi and F. Stefani, *La Participazione dell'Italia alla Guerra Civile Spagnola, 1936-39*, Rome, Ufficio Storico dello Stato Maggiore Esercito, 2 vols., in 4 parts, vol. 2, part 1, p. 481ff.; F. Bargoni, *L'Impegno Navale Italiano durante la Guerra Civile Spagnola (1936-1939)*, Rome, Ufficio Storico della Marina Militare, 1992; F. Pedriali, *Guerra di Spagna e Aviazione Italiana*, Rome, Aeronautica Militare Italiana, Ufficio Storico, 1992.

[10] Rovighi and Stefani, *La Participazione*, vol. 22, part 1, p. 481.

[11] Minstero Affari Esteri, Carteggio U.S., n.5, b.3; Rovighi and Stefani, *La Participazione*, p. 454 ff; F. Guarneri, *Battaglie Economiche tra le due Grande Guerre*, vol. 2, Milan, 1953, p. 334ff. (Guarneri was Secretary for Trade and Foreign Exchange. He warned Mussolini at the time—uselessly as it happened—that Italy might go bankrupt.) R. De Felice, "Mussolini, il Duce," pp. 773, 802 ff.

[12] De Felice, "Mussolini, il Duce."

[13] Sadkovich, *Understanding Defeat*, p. 32 ff. See also the diary of the Chief of General Staff, Ugo Cavallero, *Comando Supremo – Diario, 1940–1943*, Bologna, 1948, to be issued soon in its entirety by the Ufficio Storico dello Stato Maggiore Esercito.

[14] Emilio Faldella, *L'Italia nella Seconda Guerra Mondiale, Revisione di Giudizi*, Bolonga, 1959, p. 131. Marshal Pietro Badoglio later signed the Italian surrender and became President of the Council following the fall of Mussolini.

[15] Ibid, p. 205.

[16] Alberto Santoni, *Il Vero Traditore: Il Ruolo documentato di Ultra nella Guerra nel Mediterraneo*, Milan, 1982; *La Marina Italiana nell Seconda Guerra Mondiale: La Difesa de Traffico con l'Africa Settentrionale*, vol. 7, 2 parts, Rome, Ufficio Storico della Marina Militare, 1976.

[17] G. Giorgerini, *La Battaglia dei Convogli nel Mediterraneo*, Milan, 1977.

[18] G. Santoro, *L'Aeronautica Italiana nella Seconda Guerra Mondiale*, Milan, 1976, p. 137 ff.

[19] Ibid, p. 133 ff.

[20] S. Licheri. Of seventy German bombers, thirty were Stuka dive bombers. The Italians had a number of dive bombers nicknamed Picchiatelli. They had been built after discarding the inadequate Breda 88 and buying the license of the JU-87 Stuka, albeit with substantial modifications.

[21] M. Gabriele, *Operazione C-3: Malta*, Rome, Ufficio Storico della Marina Militare, 1975, p. 261ff. Mainly through his extensive appended evidence the author clearly demonstrates the responsibility of Rommel, Mussolini, and Hitler in giving up the attack against Malta.

[22] Montanari, *Le Operazioni in Africa Settentrionale*, p. 638; *La Difesa del Trafico con Africa Settentrionale*, Appendix 17.

[23] Montanari, *Le Operazioni*, p. 640.

[24] Ibid, pp. 660, 663.

[25] Santoro, *Aeronautica Italiana*, vol. 2, p. 319ff.

[26] Ibid, vol. 2, p. 33.

[27] Montanari, *Le Operazioni*, p. 649.

[28] Correlli Barnett, *The Desert Generals*, p. 247. Barnett gives 220,000 men for the Eighth Army. Data given here comes mainly from Montanari, *Le Operazioni*, p. 70ff.

[29] Montanari, *Le Operazioni*, see "Riassunto de Rapporto tenuto da Rommel nella riunione del 22 settembre 1942," p. 977ff.

[30] Liddell Hart, *The Rommel Papers*, p. 293.

[31] Giuseppe Mancinelli, *Dal Fronte dell'Africa Settentrionale (1942–43)*, Milan, 1970, p. 175. General Mancinelli was the Italian liaison officer at Rommel's headquarters.

[32] Paolo Caccia Dominioni and G. Izzo, *Takfir*, Milan, 1967, p. 70ff.

[33] Mancinelli, *Dal Fronte*, p. 173ff. See also the report by Lt. Colonel Izzo quoted, Dominioni and Izzo, *Takfir*, p. 171.

[34] Montanari, *Le Operazioni*, p. 978.

[35] Dominioni and Izzo, *Takfir*, p. 50.

[36] Montanari, *Le Operazioni*, p. 978.

[37] Mancinelli, *Dal Fronte*, p. 187.

[38] Santoro, *L'Aeronautica Italiana*, vol. 2, p. 331.

[39] Dominioni and Izzo, *Takfir*. Izzo was repatriated for treatment and, when he had recovered, was sent to the new paratroop Nembo Division, fighting successfully on the Italian front on the Appenines, this time against the Germans. He was wounded yet again, and decorated for gallantry.

[40] Montanari, *Le Operazioni*, p. 742.

[41] Ibid, documents.

[42] Montanari, *Le Operazioni*, Cavallero to Mancinelli, 4 November 1942, p. 799; ibid, Hitler to Rommel, p. 203; Mancinelli, *Dal Fronte*, p. 202ff.

[43] Dominioni and Izzo, *Takfir*, p. 97.

[44] Dominioni, *Le Trecento Ore a Nord di Quattara, 13 Ottobre–6 Novembre, 1942: Antologia di una Battaglia a cura di Paolo Caccia Dominioni*, Milan, 1972, p. 233ff., 435 ff.

[45] Liddell Hart, *The Rommel Papers*, p. 324ff.

[46] Ibid, p. 325. Author's translation from the original German.

[47] Tank crews.

[48] Sweet, *Iron Arm*, p. 189.

Peter Liddle

Rescuing the Testimony of the North Africa Campaign Experience

For well over thirty years the focus of my work has been the rescue and consideration of the evidence of personal experience in wartime. For most of that time my focus has been upon the evidence relating to the Second World War. Personal experience documentation offers an invaluable insight into our past. Of course it does not supplant the official record, though on occasion it can offer a substantial challenge, but it provides the researcher with the opportunity of identifying more closely with what it means for individuals to go through the experience being studied, and seldom would that have been the purpose of the official record.

By use of local, national, and international press, I have sought men and women who went through wartime experience; for most, it has been a matter of enduring or accepting it; for some, resenting it; and, for others, enjoying it. I have interrogated them rigorously by tape recording and then have attempted to persuade them to place their letters, diaries, and related papers and souvenirs into archival preservation for long-term security. Today's symposium centers upon al-Alamein or, more broadly, the North Africa Campaign, and I am deeply anxious that the evidence of the North Africa Campaign experience of men from Britain, the Commonwealth, Germany, Italy, France, the United States, and other countries involved in the war, including Egypt, should not be lost.

Why is it so important that it be saved? Most obviously because the evidence is in danger through the loss of the men and women concerned and hence their recollections—their original letters, diaries, photographs, artwork, maps, memorabilia—threatened, unless recorded, by destruction, disposal, dispersal, and disappearance. It is not just that this material has endless fascination for all of us steeped in its consideration, but also that it explains or, indeed, challenges so much that is generally accepted at a variety of levels by succeeding generations. It may be added that all too often the level of understanding is superficial and yet held with all the passionate conviction of the ill-informed. To paraphrase the protest of James MacDonald Fraser in a memoir he wrote about his service in the Burma Campaign: when he hears the campaign discussed or portrayed in media terms today, he finds it difficult to relate what is presented with the experience he shared with fellow infantrymen.

I believe we have a duty to those men and women who had experience of war to evaluate properly and make more widely known their response to the challenge it brought to them, for is not our present time simply the evolution of past times? Surely the understanding of those past times gives us a much better appreciation of our present when, of course, we are building the future for others. I have in mind our young people, their upbringing, and then their education. Judgments about the past will change with each generation, but a striving for understanding, a retention of interest and respect, should be constants.

Before placing before you some vignettes of al-Alamein experience it would seem useful to indicate some of the principles which influence me when I am talking with a North Africa Campaign veteran. This will, not least, make clear that I see such evidence as complementary to and supportive of contemporary letters and diaries and, in their absence, as a substitute of some significance.

Interviewing a North African veteran, I want to make him young again. I want to learn of his duties at the time, his routine, his reactions, his opinions, his attitudes, his relationship to his fellows and his immediate superiors and, if appropriate, those in junior rank to him, and then what he saw, did, and experienced. My questions will be within that framework and not outside it. Furthermore, I am learning all the time the context of his experience. I must not think

I hold in my hand the al-Alamein experience in that November 1942 letter or 1998 cassette recording of his recollections of the battle. It is, rather, one man's experience. He may be a gunner in the infantry, or a sapper in the crew of a tank; his responsibilities could be in mine clearance, vehicle maintenance, or whatever; but also, that man may be an Australian, a New Zealander, a South African, an Indian, a Frenchman, a Greek, an Egyptian, or an Italian or German, and this, of course, may add particular qualifications upon or distinctive significance to his memories. Then, what sort of man is he? How did such a man react to his experience? We need to bear in mind his social and educational background, his character and personality and not just those basic and, of course, significant factors such as name, rank, unit and the date of a particular experience or sequence of experiences.

The context is important in a whole range of matters. Does the al-Alamein experience lie wholly on the gritty sands of the Western Desert? Surely there is the aerial dimension too. Air operational duties and aircraft maintenance (where those gritty sands certainly are a factor) need to be within our consideration too. Then, again and again, we are reminded of the questions of seaborne supply: are not the seamen bringing supplies, the sailors protecting them from surface vessel or submarine threat, and those at sea committed to sinking those supplies not part of the North African military experience?

Our focus in this symposium is on al-Alamein, but that should not remove from consideration the siege and capture of Tobruk, the battles of Gazala or Alam al-Halfa, the westward pursuit of the Axis forces after al-Alamein, indeed the Tunisian landing of Operation Torch and the subsequent fighting. Then many determining factors in these engagements—weaponry, supply, morale, leadership—can in fact find exemplification in the experience of the soldier in the ranks. Ask a German panzer veteran about fuel shortage and conservation of supply for his tank—not for the Afrika Corps, not for Rommel, but for his tank.

Yesterday the speakers at this conference were protected in their comfortable coach journey to al-Alamein from a peril present even in the Western Desert of peacetime—dehydration. Ask an Italian, a German, a British soldier about his shortage of water in 1942, and ask him too about his desert sores, his sunburn, the dust, the daytime heat and the cold of the night as it stays in his memory, and we shall come a little nearer to understanding important factors in his October/November 1942 experience.

It is widely recorded that Montgomery concentrated upon inter-arm training as something missing previously in the British soldier's battle training. How does a British gunner veteran today or an infantryman speak of his experience here: was there a change in attitude as a result of having the role of an 'alien' arm explained and demonstrated, and then of having to cooperate?

How strictly followed were the small details of deception plans—tanks disguised as lorries, 'showing the enemy what you haven't got, concealing what you have'? Camouflage in conception, on the drawing board as it were, was one thing but what was required of lorry drivers and tank crews in concealing movement and identity in parking-up?

Can we learn from the evidence of individuals just why, at al-Alamein, there were elements of the Somme in 1916, Cambrai in 1917, 3rd Gaza in 1917, Megiddo in 1918, or Amiens in 1918? Perhaps most surprising of all, when heavy rain seriously interfered with pursuit after each side had taken heavy punishment, dare one detect a link to unpredictable weather interference, as at 3rd Ypres in August 1917?

In all my reading on al-Alamein, nothing makes me personally more uncomfortable in trying to get inside the soldier's experience than the mine fields and mine clearance. How did individuals remember doing it? Certainly it would be interesting to learn the actual mechanics of the activity, but also whether it was 'simply a job which had to be done and we had been trained to do it,' or whether there were stresses different from those endured by men engaged in other duties.

And what was it really like for an infantryman to have to move up a bare, rocky ridge to take undestroyed machine gun posts, and did tank crews really worry about the danger of immolation as a result of interior damage igniting the fuel, or was this 'something which could only happen to others'?

I am interested in the individual's mind and the emotions—the stress of command, the stress of composure so that one would not let oneself down in front of one's mates. What is it like to be winning; what is it like to be losing; what is it like not to know who is winning or losing? Were men really inspired by Montgomery's style of leadership? There is evidence on film of his informal and formal addresses. Here is the text of his eve-of-battle-written "Personal Message from the Army Commander to the Eighth Army":

1. When I assumed command of the Eighth Army I said that the mandate was to destroy ROMMEL and his Army, and that it would be done as soon as we were ready.

2. We are ready NOW.

The battle which is now about to begin will be one of the decisive battles of history. It will be the turning point of the war. The eyes of the whole world will be on us, watching anxiously which way the battle will swing.

We can give them their answer at once: "It will swing our way."

• We have first-class equipment—good tanks, good anti-tank guns, plenty of artillery, and plenty of ammunition—and we are backed up by the finest air striking force in the world.

• All that is necessary is that each one of us, every officer and man, should enter this battle with the determination to see it through—to fight and to kill and, finally, to win.

If we all do this there can be only one result—together we will hit the enemy for 'six,' right out of North Africa.

• The sooner we win this battle, which will be the turning point of this war, the sooner we shall all get back home to our families.

• Therefore, let every officer and man enter the battle with a stout heart, and with the determination to do his duty so long as he has breath in his body.

AND LET NO MAN SURRENDER SO LONG AS HE IS UNWOUNDED AND CAN FIGHT.

Let us pray that "the Lord mighty in battle" will give us the victory.

B. L. MONTGOMERY,

Lieutenant-General, GOC-in-C, Eighth Army.

MIDDLE EAST FORCES,

23-10-42.

There was a written message from the king too:

I pray that God may bless the Desert Army in the important battle which has now begun, from which great results may flow to the cause of the

United Nations in every part of the world. I have the utmost confidence
in the troops from all parts of my Empire and in their Commanders.

All my thoughts are with you.

GEORGE R.I.

Did a man feel that he was targeted personally by such exhorta-
tions? One's reflex judgement today of such a question might well
be cynically dismissive, but an assessment based on 1942 evidence
in soldiers' letters or diary references would be more convincing.
And then there is, too, the possibility of interrogating veterans on
this and other matters about their degree of confidence in the leadership at different levels of command. It might be mentioned here
parenthetically that these issues are of more than just 'antiquarian'
interest: despite seemingly accelerating technological transformation of the art and practice of war, there are timeless factors in the
relationship of leaders and led which ensure that when things are
right in this matter, men perform more effectively.

The subjectivity of personal experience evidence, contempora-
neous with a campaign or retrospective, is as self-evident as the
caution which must be used in offering generalization from such
evidence. This should be regarded as implicit in everything put forward for consideration in this paper. However, it would be perverse
if such strictures were to preclude the inclusion of examples of the
evidence which is available. By choosing a lieutenant in command
of a tank, and an infantry subaltern in command of a platoon, each
reflecting some of the turbulence of emotional reaction to battle, an
attempt is being made to tread through a historical minefield and
present this as properly representative response to the reality of the
al-Alamein experience of British soldiers.

First we have T/Major A.F. Flatow in command of 'A' Squadron,
45th Royal Tank Regiment (Leeds Rifles), writing in a letter composed with time on his hands during his troopship's return home on
leave some months after the battle.[1] He dealt first with the waiting
period:

> The evening of the 23 October came too quickly and everything was
> ready for the great effort. I have never known such an atmosphere among
> troops before. Their excitement made them sing, laugh at any silly joke,
> and work like stallions. I mentioned this to the colonel who had been in

the last war and he said it was quite usual with troops who had never been in battle before. When it is the second effort, the same excitement is noticeable but with it there is a grimness. This grimness was certainly absent on this night. A quietness came over everything; no movement was seen in the valley below us where all the 8th Armd Bde were concentrated in the same formation as we were.

Then their waiting was rudely interrupted and any confident expectations, uncertain apprehension, or worse was replaced with new immediate realities.

And then it happened. When it happened I was sitting on the outside of Sgt. Horne's Crusader trying to contact Col. George Parkes of the 47th Bn. First of all we heard the familiar hum of an aeroplane: it was fairly cloudy and visibility was not too good, and we couldn't see it. It got nearer and when it was overhead we heard the whine of falling bombs. The first four fell right in the middle of the echelon of the 8th Armd Bde and about forty vehicles went up in flames and, as these were only a few hundred yards from us, it is to be realised how we felt. I was talking to Col. Parkes at the time and we thought that the first bombs had hit his echelon. The burning vehicles lit up the whole area for yards and orders were given for the Bde to scatter. The whole organised pattern of the Bde became hopelessly mixed up and Col. Parkes had told me that Abdy Collins was doing first-class work with his sappers but that a further minefield had been found beyond the original enemy one. I was wandering about on the outside of this Cruiser, looking for Bde HQ to give the Brigadier a message about the state of affairs. The Stuka—for such it was—continued to bomb the vicinity of the fire, which was now blazing to high heaven and causing casualties. Cpl Reeves-Lawler and one or two others were killed and wounded. I had to make a further trip from Bde HQ to Col. Parkes, and on the way a bomb fell so close that the blast of it blew me off the tank onto the ground, where I cowered waiting for the remaining bombs which invariably followed the first. I was never more frightened in my life. For the first time real fear came to me—in a big way. Luckily Tpr Bailey, who was driving the Crusader, had just about pulled up and he had heard the diving scream of the plane before dropping the bombs. After the plane had passed, I ran over to some Bren Carriers where I thought some people had been hit, but here there were no casualties. By now fires of hit vehicles had sprung up round about the huge bonfire of the echelon, and more Hun planes arrived and gave us Hell. I got back to 'A' Sqdn as soon as I could and found them all scattered. I managed to contact the Troop leaders after a bit and climbed into the protecting turret of Attila. I then tried to find the Colonel, but in vain. Whilst on this errand, I passed near a blazing 15 cwt truck and on the sand near it, lit up by the flickering flamers, were three bodies stretched out—an eerie sight in the dark and I was pleased to get away from it.

From a tank to an infantry platoon and the recall of Lieutenant Ewen Frazer, No. 1, A Company, 1st Battalion Gordon Highlanders.[2] Frazer remembered spending a long day of silent introspection, isolated, immobile in trenches until nightfall allowed free movement, a hot meal, and the contemplation of the orders for the night attack.

We mustered again in silence on our startline, set out on white tapes on the desert floor in charge of our intelligence officers, Lt. Miller and Tyler, who would navigate us to our objectives, laying out tapes and signs behind them in a very orderly manner.

We were beginning to feel the night cold after the heat of the day, and becoming a prey to our thoughts. Our morale was high. We were physically and mentally strong. The unknown factor was how we would stand up individually under fire. This is said to pervade the thoughts of soldiers on the eve of their first battle. Our accoutrements must be mentioned. The weight seemed excessive to us because, apart from carrying a day's ration of food and water, an entrenching tool to dig our slit-trenches (shared between two), ammo for one's personal weapon, a private soldier's rifle and bayonet (which I preferred to the officer's revolver), we shared carrying ammo and spares for the platoon Bren gun and anti-tank rifle (which I think we later discarded). In addition, we carried a pick or shovel each and as many of the excellent Mills hand grenades as we could stuff into the pouches on our chests. Someone in our platoon of twenty-five soldiers carried the antitank sticky bomb which could blow a hole in the side of a tank. It was the size of a child's football and very awkward to carry; however, I never heard of anyone heroically stupid enough to apply it to a tank in the desert, though no doubt it was used elsewhere, in close country perhaps.

Thus we were sat uncomfortably on the desert floor in extended order at four yard intervals, companies 'A' and 'C' covering a hundred yards with rear sections behind, AWAITING THE BIG EVENT. The biggest artillery barrage (2140 hours) since the 1914/18 war opened up on time to dramatic effect. We hoped it would soften up our enemy sufficiently to gain our objective—they being dug in, we on top of the ground. We had mixed feelings. This first barrage was an anti-counter battery fire to take out the enemy's guns (2140). The second barrage we were to follow was to be a creeping one at walking pace, 100 yards to the minute, pausing at intervals on known enemy positions to enable us to overcome them before they had recovered. We duly advanced for an hour behind the 5th Black Watch to our start line proper without incident (2300 hrs). There we found a wall of shell fire in front, and our Bn. Cmdr. Nap Murray held us up for ten minutes, suspecting our own artillery falling short, which of course we knew nothing of at the time, thankfully....

I can only describe our advance and attack as a jumble of fleeting incidents. Generally we kept up our steady advance through the shell fire until forced to go to ground, when the shout would go up to keep going. Considering the amount of shells exploding among us, it amazed me how light our casualties were at that stage; soft sand no doubt helped.

Two incidents: the first Pte. Philips, an excellent soldier and friend, lost his nerve, declared himself hit, and became our first "bomb happy" casualty. We had to leave him behind. The second, our artillery officer and great friend Crosbie McTaggart, was killed beside me by a direct shell hit. He had been carrying heavy wireless gear and been unable to drop quickly to the ground. The dust (sandstorm) kicked up by shellfire was so bad and visibility so bad and fleeting, my chief concern was to keep our lines straight and keep our boys from straying off course. I am ashamed to say on one occasion I joined the hand of two of my soldiers to impress on them to stay together. A glance to my right in a shaft of moonlight showed me a section of Aussies—five or six—strung out in the best of good order, very encouraging. They were our right flanks, 9th Australian Division. Later they were to approach me when we began our attack proper and offered to put themselves under my command, saying they were lost. Rather thoughtlessly I declined and sent them on their way.

Suddenly our advance was halted in the centre by extremely heavy point-blank rifle, spandau machine gun and mortar fire, causing heavy casualties and stopping us in our tracks. Fortunately my platoon was on the flank of the enemy's position and my right-hand section, with Corp. Dunlop and Pte Neil to the fore, took them at the charge with rifle and bayonet, and killed the seven occupants and took over their position. I immediately returned to company headquarters to find Capt. James

McNeil, my Company Commander, badly and, indeed, mortally wounded and our attack grounded. I covered him with my jersey, told him the attack had succeeded, and tried to compose him. We were clearly in the killing zone of the enemy platoon's position, with the sections over the ridge bringing down accurate mortar fire on us and causing more casualties. We had to put a stop to it, so I told acting 'C' coy Cmdr. Lt. Harry Gordon to give me a short burst of Bren fire on the enemy position we could see, and I would attack it from our flank forthwith. It was quite straight forward. I threw my grenade on target, and my section rushed them with rifle and bayonet. At the last minute one or two attempted to surrender, but it was too late for them and the position was taken without further casualties.

In the same way that Flatow's tank was but one of 1,114 British tanks in the battle, Ewen Frazer was one of 150,000 British troops involved, and Crosbie McTaggart, his friend, was one of 2,400 British killed or died of wounds in the battle. Perhaps altogether 500 British tanks were lost, and 13,500 British troops were killed, wounded, or missing. These are the figures generally quoted. Significant, too, in the sense of scale, even if questionable, are the British estimates of Germans and Italians killed, wounded, or missing—55,000.

To Flatow's and Frazer's evidence should be added the testimony of the gunner, certainly, but then too of the sappers engaged in mine clearance work, those who marked and illuminated the cleared passageways and directed traffic through them, and medical staff engaged in the initial treatment of the wounded and then carrying out swiftly their procedures for evacuating casualties.

I have focused attention in my quotations upon the British soldier, but I am mindful of the evidence of his 1942 allies in the Western Desert and of his Italian and German opponents. I make no apology for returning to my opening theme; we should be concerned to rescue this material—because of its fascination, yes; because of its aid towards understanding our past, yes; because of the continued utility of what can be learned from it, yes; but because, not least, it is our past—our British, our Commonwealth, our Italian, our German past—and it is vanishing before our eyes. What a shameful abdication of responsibility if we were to do nothing to rescue what remains before it is too late.

NOTES

[1] Letter 4.6.43, Liddle Collection, the Library, University of Leeds.

[2] Typescript recollections, Liddle Collection, the Library, University of Leeds. Frazer was awarded a DSO for his part in the battle.

Ernst-Heinrich Schmidt

Refurbishing the Egyptian Military Museum at the Battlefield of al-Alamein: A Case Study in Military Museological Practice

There were three guiding principles in the internationally support-ed refurbishment of the Egyptian government museum commem-orating the battles of al-Alamein. The museum had first to explain the politico-strategic elements of the momentous events of 1942, and to show something of the complex organization and adminis-tration of desert warfare. Second was the need to show something of the daily life of the soldier in the desert beneath the scorching Egyptian sun. Then, third, from the museological point of view, it was essential to illuminate the Desert War from the side of both Allied and Axis armies.

For most ground troops on both sides, the reality of al-Alamein involved at least three months of trench warfare. In practice, this meant surviving in the dreariest region of the Western Desert—a barren place, truly desolate, a hell of sandflies, diarrhea, and dev-astating heat. For the men it was an existence lived out in constant fear of artillery fire by day and of enemy raids and machine gun-fire by night, a place whose connection to civilian life was the sin-gle track, coastal railway line. And all these hardships were to be endured on a monotonous army diet.

Yet if the privations of desert warfare at al-Alamein were a shared experience, the conclusion of the fighting brought great dif-ferences. For Allied troops the final break-through came only after twelve days of terrible fighting and with heavy loss of life. But at least for them this decisive battle marked the first British and Commonwealth victory in either the European and Mediterranean or the Far Eastern theaters of war. For the political and military leaders of the Axis powers, on the other hand, the same battles spelled an irreversible change of fortune. For them, the defeat at al-Alamein and the ending of the siege of Stalingrad in November 1942 marked the turning point in World War II. Axis capitulation at al-Alamein and Stalingrad ended Hitler's 'Orient Strategy' (see Map I), and brought into play the Anglo–Soviet Treaty of May that year, enabling the Soviet–Allied pincer advance which would ultimately bring about Hitler's downfall. And yet, as the museum itself testifies, for all the horror of desert warfare and the tremendous loss of life, these battles remain in the memory of both sides as among the few which can be recalled with sorrow but without shame.

A Museum Memorial

The exhibits at al-Alamein Museum were selected on the three guiding principles. Of first importance were the politico-strategic-military considerations of the chief former belligerent powers involved in that theater of war. Then there was the need, referred to earlier, to project the very different struggles that faced the individual soldier in the desert war and, at the same time, to honor the campaigns of both groups of combatants. In this way, the museum would complement the several beautiful memorials around the site and—in a different, though equally poignant manner—pay tribute to the fallen dead.

The present writer, for example, had seven cousins killed in action. Of these, one still lies missing beneath the sands of the Western Desert at the place where the 51st Highlanders broke through the Italian lines which had pockets of German troops sandwiched between them. Another—a pilot of a Junkers 88—was shot down over Malta, his heavy plane loaded with bombs. A third—a submariner—was bombed and sunk as his submarine made its way back through the Straits of Gibraltar after carrying out its Mediterranean mission. Now, beside each other in the German Hall, stand models of a German bomber pilot and an RAF fighter pilot.

Map 3: German War Graves in North Africa

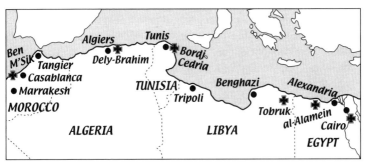

Map after Eppele after Volksbund Deutsche Kriegsgräberfürsorge and E.-H. Schmidt.

To illuminate the magnitude of both the grand-scale slaughter and the personal experience of death, victors and vanquished, survivors and relatives would be asked to contribute their reminiscences and impressions. An occasion that facilitated this was the fiftieth anniversary of al-Alamein on 23 September 1992, when veterans in their seventies and eighties, as well as many others, returned to see for themselves the graves and tombstones, the cenotaphs and memorials.

Visitors frequently remark on the appropriately distinctive national style of each of the memorials. The Commonwealth War Graves Commission Cemetery at al-Alamein, for example, sweeps out towards the desert. It is set in a garden where strands of brilliantly flowered bougainvillea contrast starkly with the ranks of neat headstones simply inscribed with names and the tellingly painful dates of young lives cut off before their prime. Since first visiting al-Alamein, I have noted the constancy with which these grounds are so beautifully maintained. In contrast, the Italian memorial of glistening, white, classical marble looks out across the Mediterranean towards Italy. Its airy portals look to the sea, whose movement accentuates the tranquility of the cenotaph with its stone walls inscribed with the names of the dead. Beyond, to the east, stands the German memorial, enclosing within its walls and listing according to the regions from which they came the names of the men who died in the desert campaign. Of the three, this is perhaps the most somber and most painful testimony to the tragedy of war.

The scale of carnage on this battlefield never fails to move. During their visit to al-Alamein, conference guests will see in the museum itself a line sketch indicating the full extent of the German war graves that lie between Cairo and Casablanca (see Map II). Indeed, the al-Alamein memorials still impart a powerfully emotive aura. "Death has a face of stone for them all, here on earth," reflected a visiting Australian, recalling perhaps the inscription on the headstones of the unidentified dead: 'Known unto God.' As one Italian priest put it, "We have the eschatology, the certainty, that they all are reunited with God."

But remember too, that among the names of the listed fallen you will find no commemoration of those surviving men whom Hitler robbed of their carefree youth. During the war they were young men of around twenty years of age. For these, who were for the most part conscripts—'civil thinking citizen-soldiers'—this war, this campaign, this battle would continue to haunt them down the decades, as for many others it will continue to do for years to come. It was in part, therefore, to create a place of remembrance for all those who took part in these campaigns that the tripartite museum experts gathered together the various artifacts, emblems, photographs, and statistics which make up the exhibits in the museum.

Getting the Project Going

These, then, were the themes written into the museum project from its beginning in 1984. The aim of the museum was "both to preserve reminiscences and to offer information on the cause, the course, and the consequences of the North Africa Campaign." This was not a challenge that could be undertaken by any single project officer on his own. We were a team, and I had good partners.

Initially the Egyptian government project for a trilateral museum was driven by Egypt's urgent need for military museological development aid, and was addressed to the "former belligerent Great Powers in the North Africa Campaigns." As my coauthor of our earlier joint report on ways of refurbishing the museum wrote in a letter to *The Times* in December 1987:[1]

> Following the visit, Colonel Dr. E.-H. Schmidt—then Director of the Wehrgeschichtliches Museum, Rastatt—and I submitted a detailed report

on the ways of modernising the museum. The Egyptian Government hoped that the participating nations would be prepared to provide the necessary funding, but neither the British nor the German Governments felt able to support such a project.

There are, I believe, plans to develop the coastline between Alexandria and al-Alamein as a tourist resort. If this happens, the battlefield and its museum would presumably become a much greater tourist attraction than it is now, and the necessary funding may then be forthcoming.

In making their appeal, Egypt hoped for contributions from each of the eleven nations that had participated in the campaigns. It was also hoped that those nations would succeed in coordinating their donations despite the long distance separating them from each other as well as from the Egyptian Military Museum at the al-Alamein site. But it took eight years of persistence by the Egyptian government before agreement was finally reached for the dispatch of the materials for preparation and display in the tripartite museum.

Countdown to inauguration began just one hundred days before the opening, by which time the three experts had received only limited allocation of government funds to buy, arrange shipment of, and prepare their historical items. With these funds they had also to design the displays and showcases. The German government paid for sixty meters of two- and three-dimensional exhibits. All had to be carefully packed for shipping and eventual display. However, once sufficient funds had been released, the focus of events shifted to Egypt, where eventually the exhibits began to arrive packed in containers and transferred by air and sea to Alexandria. Finally, just three weeks before the official opening of the newly refurbished museum, all the various items for display had at last arrived. Photographs now forming part of the author's archive of this project give some idea of the chaos from which order had somehow to emerge.

I was sometimes struck by the way in which planning and procedures for carrying out the museum project seemed to echo the planning, operations, and logistics of generals O'Connor and Rommel, the two outstanding tank commanders in the Western Desert. Indeed, the materials and skills required for the museum project had to be transposed to North Africa in pretty much the same manner as the war commanders and their supplies half a century earlier. Logistics invariably involved the same kind of calculations required for exports from Europe now as they did then.

This time though, thank heavens, it was all carried out in the spirit of international common sense, collegiality, and friendship which had grown through contacts built up between institutions and people, many of whom I knew from various congresses, symposia, visits, and correspondence. There is a camaraderie among NATO's military, and even the countries of the then-still-existing Warsaw Pact. Indeed, this extraordinary cooperation in the closing phases of the Cold War enabled me to accommodate Polish and Czech friends who wanted to contribute in some way to the museum project. Archival photographs (not included here) show the author in Prague in pursuit of relics of the Czechoslovakian Battalion at Tobruk.

But the value of the contributions cannot be measured by size or cost alone. We were naturally proud of the 8.8 antiaircraft gun transferred from Germany to Alexandria by special military cargo transport plane. But of equal importance to the display, and beyond material value, were many of the smaller items. These included, for example, a tiny parcel from Australia containing the second half of an identity tag and a letter written by a company commander aged twenty-one, informing a mother of the death of her son, aged twenty-two, killed in action at al-Alamein.

The Museum in its Local and Geographic Context

For Italian and German troops, the battles in June and July 1942 around al-Alamein, some 110 miles southwest of Alexandria and 300 kilometers northwest of Cairo, mark the high point of Rommel's Afrika Korps in North Africa. This was the nearest he was to come to breaking through the Allied lines, advancing to Alexandria and the Nile Delta, and marching the next 200 kilometers on to Cairo. Early success, however, soon turned to failure with the steady buildup of the Allied Eighth Army under generals Auchinleck and Montgomery. A second attempt three months later also failed. In October British and Commonwealth troops counterattacked, forcing the Axis troops to retreat through Libya to

Tunisia. The opening of the British and American front in the western Mediterranean forced the final withdrawal of Axis troops in May 1943.

The Strategic Seesaw, 1940–43

In 1942 al-Alamein consisted of a simple station on the Egyptian coastal railway line and a small pumping station. This was an ideal 'barrier' position: the Red Sea runs far to the south and the northern edge of the Qattara Depression, at below 134 meters, is scarcely accessible containing—as it does—wide sumps of saliferous clayforms. Finally, the Mediterranean forms a barrier to the north. This area, therefore, encloses al-Alamein at the tightest bottleneck of a funnel shape narrowing toward the east. Here the funnel is no more than sixty kilometers wide. Within this constricted area it is simple to illustrate and plain to see how Montgomery's numerical supremacy overcame the Italian–German units suffering, as one historian has put it, from 'drop by drop' logistics.

Desert Warfare

Of the various campaigns—characterized as 'strategic seesaws' by General Alan Brooke and Field Marshal Alexander and as *'der Pendelschlag'* by generals Kesselring and Warlimont—consider, for example, the Tell Issa, five times lost and five times regained between early July and late October. Here, finally, on the spot where the German memorial now stands, the Australian infantry bayoneted the last of the Axis antitank units which had thus far survived the shelling of Montgomery's thousand guns and the rolling, air-to-ground RAF support.

A short distance off is Sidi Abd al-Rahman, a desert wilderness, tabletop flat, with its wide, white shore stretching to the inviting Mediterranean Sea, an invitation to swim, however, that no soldier dare accept for fear of surprise attack from hunter fighters. This position was twice lost, twice regained, and finally taken by the New Zealanders. And yet it looks so peaceful now.

Not far away from Tell al-Aqaqir is the spot where, on 3 November 1942, the commanding officer of the German Afrika Korps used the thirty-four tanks remaining from two entire tank divisions in a last counterattack against some hundred United States–manufactured tanks under British command. Here General von Thoma watched his last four tanks endeavoring to protect the withdrawal on foot of his remaining infantry before being captured himself. On the same date at Hill 28, named for its height in meters above sea level, a German stronghold was defended to the last against the British.

About five kilometers east lay the incomparable stronghold of the British troops, first under Auchinleck and then under Montgomery. This redoubt was never taken by Axis forces, exemplifying Wellington's maxim concerning the right choice of terrain for the right use of artillery, first for defense and then for counterattack. This, it was decided, was also the best place for the Battlefield Museum.

Refurbishing the Existing Museum

There was already a military museum on this site first established by the Egyptian government in the 1960s, but exactly when and by whom I could not discover since the relevant documentation could not be found at Egyptian headquarters. My own reports on proposals for refurbishment, produced at President Mubarak's request, also went astray. In these official, confidential military reports I had set down my impressions of the Egyptian Military Museum, which I saw for the first time in 1984.

THE MUSEUM INTERIOR

In 1991 the existing museum consisted of a building of around 600 meters square and badly in need of repair. During the wet spring of 1992 water was seeping through the ceiling and falling not only on visitors but also onto exhibits and into the obsolete, unprotected, electrical installations. The cause of this key problem was the honeycomb structure of the roof, which involved cup formations being inserted between layers of concrete but upside down, creating receptacles that could not contain the buildup of water. The tripartite governments insisted on a thoroughly waterproof roof; a modern, high voltage electrical supply with a permanent connection to the main electric cable; and emergency generators. There was to be running water for the lavatories, etc., before they would consider offering material assistance, still less military objects on loan.

It was also necessary to protect the entrance and exit from sand-storms to prevent the fine nitrate-acid sand from being carried in on the soles of visitors' shoes. To do this we created windshields and a small sluice at both entrance and exit. The main sluice was to have been located just after the entrance to the Common Room, which was the reception and orientation area. However, it proved impossible to construct in aluminum and glass, not least because the carefully packed and expensively imported Belgian glass was broken while in storage outside. For the same protective reasons the glass skylights had to be closed and sealed against penetrating sand. Yellow-brown glass was bought, painted with an ultraviolet protective gel, and hidden behind thick, heavy curtains.

THE MUSEUM EXTERIOR

For the new museum, we decided that first there should be a semi-circular road approach. Then we reorganized the exterior and its immediate surroundings to give a green, welcoming, 'oasis' aspect to visitors arriving after their 100-300 kilometer trip through the Western Desert: somewhere to sit and rest, perhaps, before return-ing home. The outdoor entrance area would also provide suitable space for mounting large, heavy items for exhibition in the round, such as our 8.8 gun.

By 23 September 1992, the day of the ceremonial reopening by Marshal Tantawi, these three essential aspects were in place: the wide main entrance, the air-conditioned cafeteria, and—most vital—the new, hygienic washrooms for visitors after their long hours in a car or tourist bus. Then, for this modern museum, the 'oasis' garden outside, with a sitting area with sunshades and a playground for children. The finished project, in other words, aimed at recreation and fun with a museological lesson in military history thrown in.

THE EXHIBITS

Our next concern was the layout of the exhibits themselves, which were designed to demonstrate the politics, military history, and the reality of soldiering during the North Africa Campaign. First would come the reception room equipped for audio-visual pretour guidance. This room would contain a library with specialized books and journals on military history in Arabic, English, German, and Italian, given by the countries involved. Visitors would be first shown the guide, and plan of the museum layout, before moving on to the exhibits themselves.

As for the display cases themselves, these were unexpectedly difficult. The first architectural plan proved too ambitious for the carpenters. A second design with carefully executed drawings and detailed measurements was drawn up. However, as a result of the carpenters' interpreting centimeters as inches, the finished show-cases ended up gigantic and, in the unkind words of one of our team, fit only as 'aquariums for dinos.' At last, the third attempt bore more resemblance to the standardized vitrines that had been ordered. Eventually there were several different sizes and shapes: small, flat cases for two-dimensional exhibits; wider box-shaped ones for larger objects; very flat ones for diagrams and statistics; and one large, central, freestanding showcase for the motorbike-and-sidecar which forms the highlight of the display.

THE DIVISION OF LABOR

With just three weeks to go, all the equipment and materials were assembled, but the actual manner in which to present the tripartite exhibition had still to be decided. Later, looking through the photographs of this collaborative effort, British Prime Minister John Major remarked on the way the exhibits represented both sides at the front: the same soldiers fighting the same war in the same desert. Seeing the idea repeated in the mingling of displays of German troops in the British exhibition hall and of British in the German hall, Major added that the very sameness of those fighting men was now reflected in the cooperation of their descendants in the refurbishing of the museum. He was reminded again, he said, of the determination of the tripartite participants that the work must be done together or not at all.

For this to succeed, two problems had to be addressed: first, how to deal with visitors' initial, inevitable, psychologically based pre-conception that they are looking at pictures or reconstructions of their 'enemy'; and second, the need to empathize with the differ-ent kinds of visitors. There would be those who had themselves been touched by the war, and those—increasingly the majority—born later but who had relatives killed or involved in the war. For them the preservation of memory in the many personal artifacts is a major attraction of the museum, and the biographical theme is one the tripartite partners were anxious to preserve. This they attempted to show in the reconstruction of the life-sized figures fully uniformed in the dress of the Mediterranean and North Africa combatants.

For example, one photograph shows a cousin of the author at the outset of his service in North Africa as a machine gunner. He was later killed at al-Alamein. His antitank gun had already run out of ammunition when a Sherman tank mowed him down. Photographs show the German antitank team running short of supplies, dirty, and bedraggled. What can never adequately be conveyed in photographs, memorials, and statistics, and which should be emphasized, is the agony of the families who lost their sons. There is, in fact, no truly effective way of preserving the memory of over one hundred thousand dead of the North Africa Campaign. Only by illustrating the individual experience, which must be multiplied a hundred thousandfold, is it possible to glimpse the nature of the life of these armies in the desert, their suffering, their agony, and their deaths. In this way what the exhibits compose is less a war museum but more a 'museum for peace.'

Even at the time, the clear intention of the combatants to keep the level of suffering as low as possible was one of the outstanding features of the North Africa Campaign. Two directives marred this unwritten agreement. The first was a secret order of 9 June 1942 from Hitler regarding 'special treatment' for certain captives—a *Führerbefehl*—burnt by Rommel on receipt. The second was Montgomery's controversial 'kill order' of 14 September 1942. But generally it is the chivalrous nature of the fighting that, forty years on, dominates accounts of this campaign, and the jointly selected items on display reflect this theme: 'war without hatred,' 'the fraternity of soldiers.'

Unusual for the twentieth century, the desert war was fought mainly in areas devoid of civilian populations. Like toy soldiers in a vast panorama, these were battles fought on a largely empty battlefield in which the professional skills of soldiers and airmen could be deployed for purely military purposes. Indeed the struggle against the desert created a bond of camaraderie between the enemies evinced, for example, in the concern to see that—whenever possible—opposing troops did not suffer from lack of water or medical aid.

To end on a personal reminiscence, delegations of Australian and New Zealand veterans once asked me just before the official opening of the exhibition if I would act as their guide. Having toured the various displays and panels, these elderly men gathered round me saying, "You are a younger brother of Rommel's Germans, those men who might very well have been our own brothers and cousins." This did not seem to me to be mere sentimentality. Rather, I believe, it was the expression of a sense on the part of these men that in that war they had supported Commonwealth ideals of brotherhood; that there in the desert they had been pitted in a struggle to end Hitler's and Mussolini's criminally provoked war.

And so it may be argued that between 1940 and 1943 the North Africa Campaign was not a totally vicious war. These battles were fought without the input of the SS and without the genocide practiced in Europe behind the combat zones. If World War II was indeed—as historians suggest—the last of the great European civil wars, in this theater of war at least it was the last 'civilly' fought war of the great powers, and the al-Alamein museum is in large part a testament to that. Insofar as it was fought on each side with respect for the other, the North Africa Campaign was quite different from other theaters of war in World War II. Regrettably it was not to prove a pattern for later battles in this terrible conflict.

NOTES

[1] Boris Mollo Rastatt, Deputy Director and Keeper of Records, the National Army Museum, London, *The Times*, Letters to the Editor, 19 December 1987.

Thomas Scheben

The German Perspective of War in North Africa, 1940–42: Three-dimensional, Intercontinental Warfare

German joke current in 1945: "How can we win the next war? With Russian tanks, American airplanes and food, British ships, Italy in the camp of the enemy, and Hitler as a corporal."

Introduction

Fascination with the North Africa Campaign and the legendary figure of Erwin Rommel continues to swell the stream of studies on these subjects as much as the climactic battle of al-Alamein itself. It might not seem to make much sense, therefore, to re-examine the operational and tactical moves through Egypt's Western Desert that finally decided the outcome of the struggle. Or did they? Was it actually the series of three major battles and various encounters that finally decided the campaign? And if so, which of them during the four months between July and October 1942 was the decisive one? Was it really Operation Supercharge[1] which Montgomery launched against the battered German and Italian formations? These questions provide the basis for discussion in this paper which examines first the environment in which this battle took place, and then the circumstances that eventually determined its outcome.

Arguably, when Rommel and his depleted forces followed the retreating Eighth Army to the various elevations between the

Mediterranean coast and the Qattara Depression, the Desert Fox's chances of ultimate victory were already slim. When Montgomery unleashed Operation Lightfoot on 23 October, defeat was virtually inevitable, for it was mainly factors and events outside the immediate battlefields of Alam al-Halfa and Ruweisat Ridge or Tell Issa that decided the issue. What follows[2] is a detailed analysis of the essentials of this particular theater of operation rather than a narrative of campaigns and battles.

Challenge
THE THEATER OF OPERATIONS

Geography may be regarded as a nonvariable condition, but the strategic importance of terrain and other natural conditions is not. Their impact can change rapidly due to political or military events. German planners experienced this when Italy entered the war. A strategically almost 'dead' region guarding the southern flank of the German-controlled zone in Europe acquired an importance which some believed could prove crucial to the outcome of the war. The complex and sometimes heated debates among planners concerning what role the Mediterranean basin should be assigned in the conduct of the war supports this observation, though it cannot be discussed at length in this article.[3] It gives ample proof, however, that German planners had not previously given much thought to the dangers or potential of this region. This was largely because Hitler constantly reassured his civil and military establishment that there would be no war against Great Britain.[4]

The Mediterranean theater opened new avenues for attacking an opponent who, after the fall of France in 1940, had otherwise withdrawn from easy reach. Might it, then, have been easier to strike at the British Empire on its periphery rather than at its very core?[5] But in that case Britain equally might have used her Mediterranean possessions for an offensive for breaking the weaker partner of the Axis alliance. Their Italian partner was a focus of concern for the German supreme command. Indeed, weighing the pros and cons of Italian participation in the war, many concluded that a non-belligerent Rome was preferable.[6] In fact, Rome's economic and military deficiencies, her colonial empire consisting of three blocks[7] isolated from each other and from a mainland open to sea and air attack on almost every side, were more of a minus than a plus for the Axis. German reaction to Mussolini's entrance into the war and offer of assistance to his Axis partner was therefore less than enthusiastic.

Italy's central position in the Mediterranean, from which major British bases were under threat of attack either directly or indirectly from severance of their lines of communication, could only be made operative with appropriate military forces. The same was true for Italy's colonies which could threaten Commonwealth positions, but could also be threatened in turn—especially by an enemy which controlled the seas and could reinforce its positions on a global scale, something the Italians could not do. So the Italian position perhaps appeared stronger than it really was.[8] Nevertheless, once the occupation of Greece was accomplished and Operation Barbarossa begun, a German drive through Turkey or across the Caucasus became a realistic option, and the eastern Mediterranean then commanded closer attention from both sides.

GERMANY IN THE MEDITERRANEAN: GEO-STRATEGIC CONSIDERATIONS

However, for Hitler's grand strategy, warfare in the west was a highly unwelcome deflection from his Armageddon in the east. Whatever his plans and motives for the invasion of Russia, once he had decided upon Operation Barbarossa in late 1940, he was reluctant to dispatch forces to other theaters. Despite uneasiness about the Italian capabilities, Hitler therefore accepted Mussolini's idea of a 'parallel war' with the Alps as a borderline. Even after he was obliged to agree to intensified German intervention, his major concern was to keep the German effort as limited as possible.

When German forces were deployed, the staff planners were challenged for the first time in their history with a 'triphibian'[9] intercontinental war, where the distances over land and sea surpassed everything of that kind in Europe. Varying requirements dictated the significance of distance. All reinforcements, every buildup of ammunition and fuel stocks, had to be planned long ahead. For example, the safest route for the Commonwealth forces from London to Alexandria around Africa was six weeks longer than through the Mediterranean. Time and again Allied commanders had to take the risk of sending convoys through the Straits of

Gibraltar in order to counter emergencies or launch an attack on time.

But the Allies at least had one safe avenue of supply; the Axis had no such alternative line of communication. For the Germans, distances over land to Italy were much shorter, but there were bottlenecks: limited harbor capacities in Africa and a dangerous shipping route. Depending on Rommel's position, land transport in Africa had—at its worst—to cover a distance from Tripoli to al-Alamein which is, for example, twice as far as from Moscow to the Polish border.[10] It took a full German panzer division sixty-five days to reach Libyan soil from Germany, of which three to four weeks were necessary for the sea crossing.[11] When the Second Air Corps moved from Army Group Center in Russia to Sicily with about 30,000 men in 1941, the first units left Russia in mid-November but their first full strength air strike was not delivered until March 1942—four months later.

On the other hand, factors of time and distance became almost meaningless in the desert war itself. The British advance in 1940–41 covered 925 km in sixty-three days, while Rommel's counteroffensive in 1942 made 610 km in just fifteen days. Mobility became an absolute imperative, and non-motorized static infantry formations could not hold out against smaller, but flexible, mobile forces. Characteristically, most losses on both sides were among those who were trapped after engagements of the armored divisions and who, being unable to flee fast enough, were left behind and run over by pursuing tanks.

The tank was undeniably the dominant weapon on the desert battlefield. Its major features, a combination of mobility, firepower, and defense from fire, became even more important in a terrain where fixed lines of defense or occupation of vast territories by infantry were impossible. Consequently, terms like front, rear, or flank lost much of their importance.[12] The major target of an attack was not a position or a piece of land but enemy troops. The one who could "be there first with most"[13] in armored forces usually won the day. Natural defense lines or favorable fortified positions like Tobruk, al-Alamein, or the Sollum–Halfaya Pass were few in North Africa, and generally could serve only to hold down enemy forces temporarily by blocking important roads until mobile forces could be organized for a counterstroke. Other than that, territorial gains and losses were only important if they brought their own air force closer to major targets like the North African harbors and overseas communication lines.

Dealing with these uncommon features proved as tough a challenge for the German Supreme Command in Berlin as for the rank and file in the desert. Conditions such as these were completely new to them. Germany had no colonial tradition worth mentioning, and only very few of its regular troops had seen service in the Mediterranean climate in World War I.[14] That experience had obviously been forgotten. Also, the German soldiers of the Afrika Corps were far from being a hand-picked elite. Their later elevated status derived from their achievements on the battlefield. But when they came to Africa they arrived as regular formations from the normal stock of German draftees.[15] Plagued by poor nutrition of fatty canned meat and with uncomfortable tropical uniforms, they suffered from ills ranging from minor discomforts to serious illness. The sick rate was always high and the number of officers and men who served continuously in Africa without sick leave and recovery in Europe was small. Even Rommel's healthy constitution failed after two years.

In general British soldiers, and especially Australians and South Africans, were physically better adapted to the conditions of a desert climate than their German comrades-in-suffering.[16] Soldiers became adept at inventing their own solutions and improvisations.[17] Certainly the Allies were better off with their base in Egypt than the Axis with theirs in Libya. Egypt could provide the armies with a variety of fresh products that the barren desert of the Italian colony could not.[18] The Italians never made any serious attempt to turn their colony itself into a supply base as did the Allies with the Middle East.[19]

WHERE EFFICIENCY MATTERED MORE THAN NUMBERS

The impact of the attitudes and conduct of a very few individuals on the overall conduct of the desert war was another uncommon feature of a world war that elsewhere was decided by armies of millions. It was a theater where small numbers could be significant. Germany fielded 234 divisions in spring 1942, of which three—i.e., less than 2 percent—fought in Africa. There was never more than 10 percent of available combat air power concentrated in the Mediterranean, and the periodically higher percentage of U-Boats present there says more about the overall numerical weakness of the *Kriegsmarine*[20] than about its effort as such.

The advent of a convoy could change the overall balance of power for many weeks—sufficient for an offensive along the whole coastline—before the opponent could react. It took only fifty-five panzers, delivered at Bengazi, to turn the tide and enable Rommel in a few short days in early 1942 to drive the Eighth Army back to the gates of Tobruk. Consequently, because it took weeks to ship in the replacements, heavy losses could seriously cripple one side—or both—for quite a while. The relatively small forces and the difficulties in the need to react swiftly to adverse battlefield developments by sending reinforcements to a threatened sector was responsible for there being never more than a very small margin between decisive victory and total defeat. For example, in July 1942 Rommel triumphantly approached the Nile only to be faced with annihilation that October. Again, during Operation Crusader in November 1941,[21] each side came close to victory or defeat several times in a few days. The result was a constant shifting between long periods when almost nothing happened and short, violent outbursts of battlefield activity or long-distance movements.

The commander who knew, or felt, that he had an edge in the race for rebuilding his strength generally had the initiative and started the next round. In no other theater of the Second World War did individual field captains have such influence on the conduct of operations. A mere corps[22] or army commander could win or lose an entire campaign; he could become personally acquainted with most of his soldiers, and he himself could become the decisive factor. Nowhere else was a campaign seen as a duel between two leaders. Montgomery himself carried a photograph of Rommel in his command vehicle. When in 1941 C-in-C Claude Auchinleck dismissed his completely demoralized army commander, Alan Cunningham,[23] he probably saved both Tobruk and his field army, because Cunningham was already considering retreat from 'Crusader' when Rommel started his raid towards the Egyptian border. Simply replacing this one key figure turned the Desert Fox's potential masterstroke into one of his more debated defeats.[24]

A theater where a single division, a handful of tanks and planes, and the presence or absence of two heavy battleships or cruisers can make the difference between dominance or disadvantage is particularly sensitive to external influences. The Mediterranean was one of many areas locked into the greater war of two power blocks in an almost worldwide struggle. Thus on several occasions events on the other side of the globe helped shift the balance from one side to the other. For example, Churchill's order to withdraw ground and air forces from Libya in order to reinforce the Greek Army encouraged Rommel to launch his first offensive. Naval losses during the battle for Crete, aggravated by withdrawals from Africa to reinforce air and sea defenses against Japanese attack at the end of 1941, led to the contemplation of a complete British withdrawal from the eastern Mediterranean. Even so, by the end of 1941, while the Royal Navy was at its lowest ebb, Allied land forces successfully pursued the Afrika Corps through Cyrenaica.[25]

KNOWLEDGE IS POWER

Given sensitivity to outside events such that the sinking of a few transports or battleships could influence an entire campaign, military intelligence acquired enormous importance. In general German intelligence never could really compete with its Allied counterpart.[26] This is as true for the service itself as for the evaluation and application of data and information. The British had broken the German 'Enigma'[27] code, and the Italians had obtained an American code which provided Rommel with precise information from reports of the American military attaché in Cairo. In terms of the land war this was not of great advantage, since both sides had more or less the same knowledge as each other. This balance came to an end when the British raided the German signal intelligence company at al-Alamein and took it out, capturing all its files, signal books, etc. From then on Rommel was fighting blindfolded.[28] Montgomery, on the other hand, knew almost everything about the German dispositions, their supply problems, etc., and prepared his defense for Alam al-Halfa and his attack four weeks later accordingly.[29] One captured German general was astonished when he realized just how much 'Monty' knew about the German dispositions.[30]

Even so, surprises were possible and too much reliance on 'Ultra,' the British code-breaking operation, could be fatal. Rommel did not inform Berlin about his imminent counterattack in

1941, catching the British completely unprepared. Sometimes he ignored orders from Germany.[31] On other occasions he (and once a visiting quartermaster general) sent Berlin exaggeratedly pessimistic reports and requests about his supply situation, depicting the Afrika Corps as already on its last legs. Churchill did not understand the bargaining element behind these reports. He took them at face value, in 1941 urging his generals into premature counterattacks at Tobruk against an Afrika Corps not yet reduced to fighting with sticks and stones. As a result, operations Brevity and Battleaxe ended as hefty British defeats.[32]

While not the decisive factor in the land battles, 'Ultra' did give the British an edge in battles for supply routes. Knowing timing and routes of convoys and even individual shiploads gave them ample opportunity to concentrate attacks on decisive targets. It was no accident that all German tankers for Africa were sunk in summer 1942. In consequence, Rommel had neither enough supply for swift mobile operations when he attacked at Alam al-Halfa, nor for mobile defense when Montgomery responded. And the Englishman knew that Rommel was denied the superior flexibility and mobility of his panzer formations because of a lack of fuel.[33]

ENTENTE NON-CORDIALE

Events of the late thirties had brought the two major European fascist dictatorships together in an alliance determined, at least temporarily, by a convergence of interests and the exaggerated nationalism of their ideologies. It lacked any real sympathy among either their peoples or major parts of their elites.[34] Both cherished negative stereotypes of each other as a result of having fought on different sides in World War I. But while Hitler at least had a positive attitude towards Italian fascism, the Duce disliked not only the Germans but also their Führer, while envious of both for their political and military achievements.[35]

There was, then, no truly fertile ground for close political and military cooperation in which both sides would have had to throttle back their egotism in favor of the joint effort. The inability to do so was also a result of the personalities of the two leaders. Both reflected the extreme nationalist ambitions of their ideologies. In personalized rule, where both the Führer and the Duce reserved all important decisions for themselves, their highly erratic, neurotic personalities had a heavy impact on their overall cooperation as allies. In addition, or possibly in consequence, neither the military leadership nor the diplomatic service of either country was able to create mechanisms for mutual decision making or for the formulation and implementation of strategy. Interservice cooperation did not work smoothly among the Germans and was almost nonexistant among the Italians. German–Italian cooperation was difficult at all levels, and cooperation across national and service boundaries out of the question. Cases where cooperation worked on the lower levels can mostly be traced back to individual efforts of two conciliatory natures finding themselves counterparts by accident.

UNPREPARED FOR WAR

The Regia Aeronautica[36] was numerically the strongest air power in the Mediterranean and technically the most advanced Italian service. However, differences in equipment and doctrine made interoperability with the Luftwaffe almost impossible. Its overall efficiency as compared with either the RAF or the Luftwaffe was low.[37] Thus, when the Luftwaffe handed over the campaign for Malta to the Italians, the British very quickly forced the Regia Aeronautica onto the defensive.

For the Germans the most crucial factor was the Regia Marina.[38] The Afrika Corps depended completely on Italian willingness and ability to provide transports and escorts for the supply across the sea. This dependency was a source of uneasiness in the German Supreme Army Command (the *Oberkommando des Heeres,* hereafter OKH) from the very beginning,[39] and was the source of constant trouble and friction for the duration of the campaign in Libya and Egypt. Even when the fall of France removed one major Allied navy from the game the Regia Marina, whose officers and men suffered something of an inferiority complex, never challenged the Royal Navy's control of the Mediterranean. Early on the Royal Navy had succeeded in breaking the Regia Marina's morale beyond recovery, and the Italian navy maintained only a defensive attitude, investing all its resources and resolve into the defense of the convoy routes to North Africa.

However, their low morale resulted in part from real disadvantages in terms of technology and training.[40] Their submarine fleet, the largest in the world, was outperformed by the German U-Boats even in its own waters.[41] Having no air arm, the navy had to rely on air support from the Regia Aeronautica. Without a substantial force of torpedo and dive-bombers,[42] and with faulty air reconnaissance, they enjoyed none of the usual advantages of land-based air support when operating in their own littorals. Consequently, even if they reached a naval battle, Italian bomber crews often distributed their payload equally amongst friend and foe.[43]

As for the Italian army, after twenty years of fascism, what little equipment it had was mostly obsolete, rendering it less efficient than its predecessor in 1915.[44] The artillery consisted of pieces from the First World War. Its tanks were no match for any European opponent, while antitank (AT) and antiaircraft (AA) components were almost nonexistant. An average of about 150 motorized vehicles was available per infantry division. Accordingly, the tactical and operational thinking of the Italian officer corps was an echo of World War I, leading to heavy losses in frontal attacks against fortified positions.[45] Similarly Marshal Rodolfo Graziani, C-in-C in North Africa,[46] never thought of assembling a mobile force for a fast surprise move into Egypt, relying instead on a mass of slow-moving infantry. The whole outfit was possibly fit for a colonial war, but failed even against minor European opponents like the Greeks.[47]

Italian soldiers often fought in a lackluster, unenthusiastic manner. Given the inferiority of their equipment and frequently inept leadership, their numerous deeds of individual dash and heroism are all the more remarkable. In a modern war, however, equipment, training, and doctrine are the determining factors.[48] Moreover, two decades of constant, militaristic, fascist propaganda had not succeeded in turning Italy into a warrior nation for which war is ultimately the highest form of existence and self-realization.[49]

The industrial base, especially the armament industry, was not of a capacity or standard to equip a twentieth-century army. It was incapable of simultaneously producing innovative designs and replacing heavy losses.[50] Great Britain was able to match three years of Italian aircraft production in one month. All this was no secret, at least not in Rome and Berlin.[51] Count Galeazzo Ciano mocked that "with that army, we can at best declare war on Peru."[52] Mussolini was realistic enough about the situation of the armed forces and duly informed Adolf Hitler—as the Führer already knew—that Italy could not be ready for a major war before 1941, 1942, or possibly 1943.[53]

A RUSTY PACT OF STEEL

By invading Poland without consulting Italy first, Hitler violated the Pact of Steel only weeks after its conclusion, and was paid back by Mussolini in the same currency. Behavior like this set the tone of the alliance throughout its existence.[54] The Duce used the early outbreak of the war as a reason to stay out for the time being in order to continue his armament program. The surprising success of the campaign in France, however, made participation imperative.

Mussolini had long cherished somewhat vague ideas of how to lead Italy, and himself, to greatness. Though lacking a clear program or strategy of how to achieve his goals, his major objectives were none the less the creation of a colonial empire and a predominant position in the Mediterranean. Sooner or later conflict with France and England as the most important players in the Mediterranean and Africa was unavoidable and Germany his only possible ally. In such an alliance Italy could only ever play second fiddle. Now convinced that the Reich would ultimately win the war, Mussolini had to enter on Hitler's side, in order to gain Italy's share of the spoils. On 10 June 1940—even as France sued for peace—Italy entered the war, attacking French positions in the Maritime Alps but without gaining much ground.

Most of Mussolini's moves during the war were motivated by an almost neurotic fear of losing prestige and influence in relation to his superior, half-hated, half-admired partner. Nazi foreign minister Joachim von Ribbentrop made it clear that booty would be shared in relation to input. Thus Mussolini would need "a few thousand casualties to obtain a seat in a European peace conference."[55] Like most observers, Mussolini believed that the fall of France had already concluded the war in Europe with an Axis victory. His entry into the war was "opportunistic":[56] the aim of this "cautious adventurer" was great benefit at small cost.[57]

But boarding the train just before it reached the station had sudden and grave consequences: roughly a third of the Italian merchant fleet was immediately interned in Allied harbors and lost for military transportation. A coup de main against Malta, as proposed in a staff study of 1936,[58] and possible surprise attacks against other British naval bases were not carried out. In the peace negotiations with France the Axis failed to secure a foothold in Tunisia, and the Italian strategy of avoiding war with Great Britain because of Italy's vulnerable 7,000 km of coastline was thrown overboard.[59]

In reckless fashion the entire Italian conduct of war was driven more by consideration of how it would influence Italy's position after the war than by the more obvious aim of first winning it. The abortive attack on Greece was done for the sake of winning an easy victory somewhere.[60] The dispatching of Italian submarines into the Atlantic and of several air crews to the Battle of Britain, followed by the dispatch of a whole army into the Russian campaign, were each triggered by Mussolini's overweening ambition.

He failed in all these ventures. By not concentrating his available resources against the most dangerous foe, he was dealt blow after blow by Britain.[61] In early 1941 the Italian colonies in East Africa were lost, the forces in Libya collapsed, and the Greeks threatened to drive the Italians out of the Balkans. Instead of gaining influence, Mussolini became increasingly dependent on German military and economic assistance. In 1940 and 1941 the Duce evaded surrender to the Allies and the collapse of his regime only by accepting German domination.[62] Inside Italy these misfortunes discredited the fascist regime that had drawn much of its legitimacy from imperialism and expansionism. Instead, failure generated political opposition. Unlike Hitler and the Nazi leadership, Mussolini and the Italian people did not perceive themselves involved in a titanic life-and-death struggle which could only end in ultimate victory or total annihilation. The Duce never really understood the true nature or roots of national–socialist ideology,[63] and tried several times to convince Hitler to make peace before it was too late.[64] Like the Italian people, he was ready to go only so far, because they were fighting for rational, if overly ambitious goals. With disaster in North Africa and the annihilation of the Italian expeditionary army in Russia in 1942 and 1943,[65] Italian loyalty reached its limit. The Axis finally broke.

IT TAKES TWO TO TANGO

The efficiency and quality of an army cannot be evaluated in absolute terms. Assessment is valid only in relation to the performance of an opponent. Victory and defeat are not only functions of an army's actions but also dependent on the enemy's response. Applying Clausewitz's observations on war, it may be said that the longer hostilities last, the more any war or battle becomes a series of mistakes. The stronger side can afford more mistakes and thus will ultimately win. Germany's performance can be estimated only after consideration of the British and Commonwealth forces.

GRAND STRATEGY

Two centuries of involvement in Mediterranean affairs did not make the British supreme command immune from committing grave errors. However, the importance of maintaining the imperial position in the Mediterranean basin was always recognized and the priority assigned to this theater was second only to that of the North Atlantic.

With the most dangerous opponent out of reach on the European continent, the weaker of the Axis partners could only be attacked from positions in or south of the Mediterranean Sea.[66] The fact that the same was true vice versa might have put the Commonwealth on the defensive for a while, but at least Churchill was confident that he would regain the initiative. In this respect he found a congenial partner in Admiral Andrew Cunningham. Representing the best traditions of the Royal Navy and labeled Britain's "greatest sailor since Nelson,"[67] he took the initiative at sea, rarely letting it slip out of his hands, and then only under the most adverse conditions. Both admiral and prime minister understood the importance of maintaining control over the central Mediterranean, and knew that Italian superiority there must be contested to the utmost. Once lost, the two guard positions of the Mediterranean—Gibraltar and Suez—would become vulnerable to an enemy who had uncontested freedom of maneuver in this central, strategic position. When the army and the RAF found the defense of Malta untenable,[68] the decision to continue the defense of Malta was mainly due to the resolve of these two men.

One of the greatest strategic blunders of the war was the British intervention in Greece in 1941. Most of the troops assigned to the support of Greece had to be withdrawn from Libya where General Richard O'Connor's offensive was still in full swing. Until then, with German aid still far away and only some Italian infantry divisions of doubtful combat value between the British spearheads and Tripoli, O'Connor's complete victory had been only weeks away. This colossal error of judgment enabled Germany to hold on in North Africa. The Germans were now able to build up their strength faster in southeastern Europe than the Empire could,[69] while the British could neither chase the Italians out of Africa nor defend Greece. This decision prolonged the war in the Mediterranean for two more years.

MILITARY STRATEGY AND OPERATIONS

Unlike the Germans, the top brass of British military services was trained to perceive its mission as an integrated venture. For them the perspective on operational thinking was always intercontinental and integrated with all other branches of service.[70] This strategic doctrine derived from the Napoleonic Wars with a touch of World War I. It said that while Great Britain had insufficient manpower to maintain armies as strong as the continental powers, it had a small army, but a strong navy "using sea power to hold the enemy with the minimum of force along the widest possible circumference, while concentrating striking strength at the point where it could most effectively be used."[71] With increasing speed and mobility of land forces this applied no longer. But it took two costly defeats in Greece and Norway to prove that times had changed.[72]

Likewise, this strategy was not applicable in the Mediterranean. British forces had to make a stand against an altogether stronger enemy. It was therefore thanks to the Royal Navy and Royal Air Force, aided by the geographic conditions, that the force the Axis could deploy and maintain across the Mediterranean never reached a size the Commonwealth could not match. Time and again it could even achieve numerical superiority—something unthinkable on the European continent. Transforming Egypt into a major place of arms, building up strong forces there, and maintaining them in the field was a logistical achievement of its own.

BATTLEFIELD CONDUCT

The best strategic software, however, is useless if the military hardware is not up to the standards. The performance of the British services was by no means uniform and, in an integrated conflict with complementary roles, the achievements of one will usually not leave the others untouched. Fortunately for the Allied side, control of the sea was a crucial element, and the Royal Navy achieved its mission. From the beginning their naval forces were superior to the Italians'. Even in striking range of major Italian naval bases the Royal Navy operated as if there were nothing like a Regia Marina or a Regia Aeronautica.[73] The most dangerous enemy of British ships was the Luftwaffe, which was constantly able to dispute British control of the sea. The lack of a strong land-based air arm plagued the Royal Navy[74] as it did her opponents.

But despite the air threat, the Royal Navy never shied away from supporting their land forces. They carried supplies to besieged positions like Malta or Tobruk and evacuated troops from Greece and Crete because, as their C-in-C Andrew Cunningham put it, "it takes three years to build a ship, but three hundred to build a tradition."[75] Similarly the Royal Air Force always kept a high morale and never lost their spirits even under highest enemy pressure[76]— especially the fighter pilots flying technically inferior planes against the Luftwaffe. The RAF's strategic deployment of striking power, the selection of targets, and the assignment of priorities, as well as the composition of forces, was definitely superior to that of the Luftwaffe and infinitely so to that of the Regia Aeronautica.[77]

At least until the Battle of al-Alamein, the weak spot in the British defense of the Mediterranean was its army. Only for brief moments in the summer and winter of 1941 was Britain in danger of losing the war at sea, and temporary German domination of the skies was always brittle and successfully challenged. It was the army in the desert that suffered some of the worst defeats of British history and whose poor performance brought the British position there to the brink of collapse.

As in the First World War, the Germans had nothing but praise for the performance of the Commonwealth infantry,[78] with the Australian defenders of Tobruk attracting most admiration.[79] Unfortunately the decisive weapon in desert warfare was the tank. Wrongly designed tanks and a mix of different types that could not deal with advanced German tactics gave the Germans a slight technological edge in tank warfare and antitank (AT) equipment. This gap, however, was not in itself sufficient to be the decisive factor.[80] More important was the deployment of mobile forces in a way that permitted the Germans to beat far superior British forces in open battle so long as enemy air superiority could at least be neutralized.

But the most striking problem was the incompetence of British middle ranks in adapting to changing conditions on the tactical and operational level. It took them more than two years to discover that the Germans did not fight tanks with tanks. Instead they had developed a sophisticated interaction between mutually supporting AT guns and tanks.[81] This meant that attacking British tank units were worn down by fire from covered AT positions until the panzers found the right spot for a shattering counterattack. Instead of developing similar, combined tactics of artillery fire and infantry support against the German AT positions, British tanks lined up like medieval cavalry and then charged frontally ahead![82] The result was that during Operation Battleaxe British tank units suffered eight times the losses of the German panzers.[83] Another example of the slow learning curve of British officers was their surprise at the unconventional employment of the famous 8.8 antiaircraft gun against their tanks at Gazala[84] two years after their first encounter of this kind in France.[85] Lip service to combined operations was paid in the handbooks but rarely applied,[86] and many officers were too arrogant to acquire knowledge of technical details of their tanks. This, not surprisingly, determined their capabilities in battle.[87]

The British forces in Egypt were excellently prepared to employ mobile tactics of small columns against numerically superior but clumsy Italian infantry formations, and succeeded perfectly in 1940.[88] The appearance of massive German panzer formations using an advanced, combined-arms doctrine, however, required faster-than-lightning cavalry-style raiding tactics.[89] Weaknesses in division and corps operations were mercilessly brought to daylight when uncoordinated, piecemeal attacks of individual and unsupported brigades were fought off with appallingly high losses by heavily outnumbered panzer formations.[90] It was Churchill who held the army and theater commanders responsible for the situation in North Africa. Yet none of his reshuffles lead to a change because the problems were located in the military middle ranks.[91]

The common sense of the men in the trenches could have enlightened the prime minister,[92] but it was Montgomery who analyzed the Eighth Army from top to bottom. He was also given the time—by Churchill and inadvertently by Rommel—and the authority to apply the necessary changes and set up a training program.[93] Despite being satisfied with his accomplishments, 'Monty' remained cautious. His design for the battles of Alam al-Halfa and al-Alamein reflected both the strengths and weaknesses of his army. He carefully avoided unleashing his tank divisions in a fluid battle against the panzers until their fighting power was broken by the fire of his powerful artillery and RAF bombs and their field fortifications had been penetrated by his first-rate infantry.[94] Though he never admitted it, his abstention from a counterstroke at Alam al-Halfa and his reluctant pursuit of the retreating Panzer Africa Army after Supercharge was probably caused by the fear that his tank formations might be trapped again by the resourceful Desert Fox and his experienced panzer leaders.

Response
DIPLOMACY, STRATEGY, AND WAR: POLITICAL OPTIONS

A war involving not merely an ally on whom one's own effort partly depended, but involving also the service branches of both nations in a complex manner, required careful coordination at all levels, not least because diplomatic as well as military questions were involved. This was especially true in the opening stages of the Mediterranean war. Between the capitulation of France in June 1940 and the German invasion of Russia a year later, Germany had to consider all these in her overall strategy towards Great Britain.

But Britain refused to accept defeat, continuing the war single-handed though now backed increasingly by the USA. The only battlefields where British land forces could be engaged were her possessions around the Mediterranean, and this was also the only stretch of water where the Royal Navy could be engaged by Italy with some chance of success. Italy had entered the war in order to cut some meat out of France and possibly expand its colonial possessions in North and East Africa at the expense of France and Great Britain. Given strong anti-British sentiments, the establishment of the nationalist Vichy government, and a fascistic regime in Spain[95] that owed its existence to massive Italian and German military assistance during the Spanish Civil War, there were other possible partners for Italy. Once Germany joined Italy in the Mediterranean, the British position in the western and central Mediterranean at Gibraltar and Malta would become untenable.[96]

Still flushed with his success in France, Hitler approached both Vichy France and Spain. But each had their domestic reasons for shying away from military conflict. Each of them, as well as Italy, wanted to make territorial gains at the expense of the other, caring more about how to share the lion's skin than how to catch him. Few professional diplomats could have succeeded in persuading them. Certainly neither Adolf Hitler nor his foreign minister Joachim von Ribbentrop had the patience or skill to do so. The longer the negotiations dragged on, the more it became obvious that Germany was still far from victory: London did not surrender, the Battle over Britain was called off, and the landing in England was postponed.

STRATEGIC OPTIONS

With or without Madrid and Vichy there still was Rome. The Duce had now entered the war, and Italy held several positions from which the British possessions in and around the Mediterranean could be threatened. In 1940 some German naval planners, including Admiral Raeder and others in the OKH[97]—the Supreme Army Command—proposed shifting the center of gravity into the Mediterranean to drive the British out, weaken Churchill at home, and thus force London to ask for terms.[98] The reason for this controversial proposition was that no comprehensive plan for a protracted war against the Empire had ever been prepared.[99] Neither were there any German–Italian plans for any sort of joint operations.[100] At this point there was a standoff: Germany had insufficient air and naval forces to mount a serious threat to England, while Britain had no army that could attack German-controlled Europe.[101]

In the Mediterranean it soon became obvious that German military capacity could not dislodge Great Britain from its strongholds. Important operations like the occupation of the almost undefended[102] island base of Malta never materialized; others like the invasion of Egypt were grinding to a halt and, once Churchill had reinforced Cunningham's fleet, the Empire was prepared to strike back in spite of the German presence in the English Channel.[103]

In autumn 1940 the OKH sent General von Thoma[104] to Libya to study the conditions for a possible German assistance. He concluded that four German panzer divisions were the most that could be supplied. A panzer corps consisting of one motorized infantry and two panzer divisions with air support would be sufficient to drive the British out of Egypt once and for all.[105] Postwar analysts have endorsed his conclusion.[106] Mussolini, anxious to preserve prestige, refused any German involvement. Four months—and with them possibly the only opportunity to win the North Africa Campaign—had been wasted.

Two months later, Lieutenant General Richard O'Connor's brilliant riposte left Mussolini no choice. The whole of North Africa was at stake. Meanwhile, however, Hitler had made the most crucial decision of his career. Whatever else he did in the coming months was subordinate to his grand design. Every effort had now to be concentrated on Operation Barbarossa, because victory over Stalin was the key to everything. Great Britain was to lose her last potential ally on the continent. The Reich would gain access to unlimited resources, including oil, and whole divisions would be freed up to campaign wherever necessary. Nobody in Germany or—what is often forgotten—in the western world, possibly not even Stalin himself, would have given a penny for the survival of Soviet Russia against a full-scale German onslaught. To this end, every other theater of war would get just enough forces to hold out, and the Red Army would be destroyed in about six weeks, i.e., at latest by September 1941.

After 'Barbarossa' a readjustment of the armament program and then re-equipment and redeployment of the Wehrmacht would surely enable the Reich to secure vital positions against a possible Anglo–American coalition.[107] This then was the strategy until late 1942 when Hitler still believed he could win the war in Russia with his second offensive. He therefore disregarded alternative solutions to the Russian strategic cul-de-sac offered by unconventional generals like Rommel.

Meanwhile, Hitler ordered a division-size force, the Fifth Light Division, to Africa to augment Italian defenses in Tripolitania. Mainly tank and antitank formations were needed to support the Italian infantry divisions against British tank attacks. The Tenth Air Corps of the Luftwaffe had to safeguard Axis Mediterranean traffic from British attack. For purely political reasons Hitler wanted to alleviate the political crisis of fascism in Italy following its series of defeats on land and at sea which had left the Italian army in North Africa blown to smithereens. Rommel's task was therefore defensive: block any further advance of the enemy and at least maintain the status quo. It is a tradition deeply rooted in the Prussian–German doctrine of leadership to order a subordinate commander what to do but not how to do it. That is, in carrying out his mission, he is left to his own devices.[108]

Rommel needed only a few weeks to come to terms with desert conditions. He concluded that static defense in a desert without natural defense positions and an open southern flank was not promising. Sooner or later the British would build up sufficient strength to overwhelm any defensive line. He expected to destroy at least a part of the opposing forces by offensive, pre-emptive action and thus break out of his defensive position. Displaying his customary vigor of pursuit, he exploited his immediate success to the hilt. Unaware of the pending Balkan invasion and 'Barbarossa,' he intended to solve the North African problem with one blow.[109] While the OKH tried to tighten the reigns for its major venture in 1941, Hitler's immediate military advisers supported Rommel's offensive approach.[110]

COMMANDERS AND COORDINATORS

Rommel was able to ignore his orders and exceed his authority largely because he was surrounded by a miasma of conflicting interests, no clear responsibility, and lack of concise operational plans. The personality and achievements of his favorite general fascinated Hitler, who was erratic and often contradictory on paper or in action himself. He permitted himself to be dazzled by Rommel's lightning strikes over the map, and thus overruled his own earlier decisions. In a theater with vast distances and limited resources, where careful planning and consequent execution were of crucial importance, the Führer and his Desert Fox created crises which later they were unable to solve.

Nazi propaganda painted the image of the Führer as a man of energetic resolution, fanatic determination, and iron will. The reality, as his military advisors found, was very different. Hitler tended to drag his feet about important military decisions, and developments in the field often outpaced Hitler's speed in decision making. At times his hesitance over military predicaments cancelled or limited the options. The complicated, politico-military framework of the Mediterranean campaign needed careful attention, something Hitler avoided whenever possible. Studious, systematic military thinking[111] was simply not his cup of tea.[112]

And yet he concentrated more and more responsibilities in his own hands. He was the political head of state and supreme commander of the armed forces, and from December 1941 took over the command personally. Notwithstanding a workload that would have overburdened more systematic leaders, Hitler delegated nothing. As a result of his not being able to do all that was needed, some of his army commanders gained the impression that they had no supreme commander at all.[113] In the Mediterranean war, with its intricate political and military structures, coordination was indispensable. Hitler's leadership, however, was based on the principle of divide and control and did not encourage coordination or cooperation, fostering instead egotism and the separation of different services.[114] There was no equivalent to a 'C-in-C South' commanding all the Italian and German forces.[115] Without such a moderator, the various army, navy, and air headquarters were unable to develop and implement strategies, plans, or operations with Hitler's OKW *(Oberkommando der Wehrmacht)*.[116] Hitler was therefore now unable to utilize fully the most efficient of military machines that had defeated every opponent between 1939 and 1942.[117] In the end this disparity between the military capacity of the Wehrmacht and its ability to win in two world wars has its roots here in the organizational capacities of the German politico-military elite.

Since neither an overall design for the conduct of the war nor a special one against Great Britain existed, improvisation became the method and the lowest possible level of involvement the guideline. This erratic formula for the Mediterranean war sometimes squandered Hitler's available forces. In autumn 1940 three divisions and a few aircrews would have been sufficient to end the campaign once and for all. Half a year later more than these forces were barely sufficient to stem the pending catastrophe. A major short-term operation in the Mediterranean was rejected because of the concentration on Barbarossa. A *mare nostrum*[118] under Axis control would actually have aided an early start to their Russian Campaign: there would have been no Balkan Campaign. Lack of supplies and air support aggravated by inconsistent decision making led in 1942 to the eventual loss of North Africa. Where before four German divisions were sufficient to defend southern Europe on African soil, now ten times that number were not enough to protect the 'soft underbelly' of Fortress Europe against later Allied invasions.

In the end lack of planning was also responsible for missing the second, and probably last, chance of winning a decisive victory between Gibraltar and the Suez Canal. Triggered by political events in Yugoslavia and Mussolini's disastrous campaign, two German armies rolled through the Balkans while Rommel campaigned between Tobruk and the Egyptian border. Simultaneously, but uncoordinated with the German advance, an anti-British revolt led by nationalist officers broke out in Baghdad. The Vichy governor of Syria permitted small numbers of German reinforcements to be airlifted via Aleppo to Baghdad, thus suggesting Syria as a possible link for a German advance into the Middle East.[119] This became even more plausible when German paratroopers descended on Crete and the Luftwaffe inflicted losses on the Royal Navy equivalent to a major naval battle.[120] Churchill expected them to continue some sort of 'island hopping' via weakly guarded Cyprus.[121] This pincer movement against the British position in the Middle East looked a perfect strategic design,[122] but was only a coincidence of favorable events and not exploited by the reluctant, Russia-oriented Hitler. According to Winston Churchill, Hitler "certainly cast away the opportunity of taking a great prize for little cost in the Middle East."[123]

The OKH itself was not prepared to capitalize on the opportunity. Hitler, shocked by his losses in Crete, temporarily lost confidence in further airborne assaults and did not use that costly occupation either to continue the advance[124] or to explore the offensive potential of Crete as an offensive air base.[125] Nor did Hitler ever seriously consider the alternative use of the German 'Green Devils'[126] against Malta in 1941[127] even though by spring 1942, according to their commander, the paratroopers had recovered from the losses in Crete and the winter's battles in the east and would have been ready for Malta.[128]

This little island with the size and population of a major European city, Britain's 'unsinkable aircraft carrier' in the Mediterranean, became a focal point in the whole campaign. Strategically it was the link between the British bases at the eastern and western entrances. But its value was doubtful because it was in striking range for whatever Italy might have flying or swimming around Sicily. Nevertheless it became a "thorn in Rommel's side."[129] Nearly everything which was necessary to wage war in Libya had to be shipped or flown in from Italy. The harbor capacities were a major limiting factor since their capacity was barely sufficient to handle the amount of goods required to keep not only Italian and German troops in the field but also the Italian civilian colony.

Another problem was the distances between the front and the harbors, such as Tripoli, which had the highest capacity, or even Bengali or Tobruk with their more limited facilities. Depending on where Rommel was, his transport columns consumed as much fuel in their own movements as they delivered to the front—or even more. During the Battle of al-Alamein 20,000 tons of supplies could not be shipped to the front where troops were showing signs of malnutrition.[130] The whole chain of supply was extremely brittle and vulnerable to the slightest interruption. Malta, besides being a base for attacks against harbors, coastal shipping, and land transport in North Africa, and for air and commando raids[131] from bases in Egypt, also provided a major jump-off point for raids against the Axis' supply line. From here bombers, light surface vessels, and submarines harassed the convoys. Air attacks against harbors in Sicily, southern Italy, and Libya started from here too.

By 1941, no longer able to sustain the war of attrition forced upon him by the British offensive, Rommel was forced to retreat from his positions around Tobruk as a result of Axis material losses and lack of replacements. Hitler's attitude of only reacting to disaster instead of also reinforcing success meant this setback served as an incentive to almost double the available air force in the Mediterranean. He did this by withdrawing the 2nd Air Corps from Russia. Its appearance restored Axis air and sea control over and around Malta in early 1942, and after four weeks of intensified air attacks against the island, Malta was silenced. Meanwhile, plans and preparations had been made for an air- and seaborne invasion of the island. Rommel, who had advanced to the Gazala line, was set to destroy the British forces there, take Tobruk, and then consolidate his position. Meanwhile most of the Luftwaffe was to reconcentrate at Sicily in order to support the invasion of Malta. With the supply lines open, a reinforced Rommel could renew his offensive and advance into Egypt. But after the fall of Tobruk, when Rommel had the Eighth Army on the run, he refused to stop his advance. The Desert Fox smelled victory—if he was permitted to pursue the beaten British relentlessly to Alexandria and beyond. With Alexandria in hand, the possession of Malta would be meaningless. Supply then could be drawn directly to this most effective harbor on the African coast, far beyond the reach of any forces on Malta.[132] Hitler, who never liked the idea of another airborne assault and did not trust the Italians to press it home, followed Rommel's plan.

As soon as the pressure from Second Air Corps was removed, Malta regained its strength, and when Rommel launched his last desperate offensive at al-Alamein, the RAF and Royal Navy were as active as ever before. Whether an assault on Malta could have succeeded or not is an open question.[133] No one, not even the resourceful air strategist Kesselring, understood that assault could probably be replaced by a total blockade of supply. What Germany tried to do with England on a gigantic scale through wolf packs in the North Atlantic could have been achieved more easily against a small island fortress.

All fuel and ammunition had to brought in, and Malta was always a net importer of food. The German crews observed that the fire of the AA guns slackened in the progress of summer 1942. Had not Operation Pedestal, despite heavy losses, resupplied the defenders with oil and ammunition, the island would have been forced to surrender.[134]

Whether the fall of Malta would have changed the outcome of the campaign is another disputed issue. The holding of Malta certainly had saved many irreplaceable transports and tankers from sinking and freed between 300 and 400 planes for use in other trouble spots. In addition, planning of moves and campaigns would have been much easier and more reliable with a secure supply line. With Malta secure, Great Britain always had an edge—as had Montgomery—in rebuilding the strength of its army in the desert and the ability to strike the harder blows. Montgomery used this advantage to the utmost in the decisive battles of 1942.

The Hardware of Warfare
THE KRIEGSMARINE

The German navy was the smallest of the three services. Since Hitler had not anticipated war against France and the Anglo–American naval powers before the end of the forties, Germany's few capital ships could not challenge the Royal Navy on the high seas. As C-in-C Admiral Erich Raeder put it, his navy would "know how to die gallantly" when the time came.[135] As it turned out, the Regia Marina could not do much better. The Mediterranean, however, offered different conditions from the open sea. Having air and naval bases nearly everywhere in striking range of every point inside the basin, small units like destroyers and fast-attack boats could be employed to considerable effect, as could sea- or airborne mines.[136] The Germans shipped a flotilla of such units through the French canal system, whose shallow waters were in many places a deathtrap for submarines. German U-Boats managed none the less to conduct some spectacular feats against the Royal Navy, while British submarines operated against Axis convoys. When Hitler ordered the reinforcement of the U-Boats to deal with the convoy crisis in 1941 and 1942, Karl Dönitz[137] had to comply. Being short of boats for the decisive Battle of the Atlantic, the main theater for the German navy, he resisted the withdrawal of his sea wolves for what he considered a mere sideshow.[138]

However, the Mediterranean being an inland sea, air power became a crucial factor in naval war. Here British naval superiority could be broken from above.[139] Late in 1941 it became clear that even the strongest British battleships could not hold out against determined air attacks. Without a fleet air arm like the British, the Kriegsmarine was dependent on the support of the Luftwaffe. The disadvantage of not having a specialized air arm for air-to-sea warfare became obvious to most other navies during the thirties, but the relevant conclusion was not drawn in Germany.[140]

Gifted with a few naval strategists capable of thinking of war in worldwide dimensions, planners drew up ambitious strategic

Map 4:

Hitler's 'Orient Strategy,' June 1941–November 1942

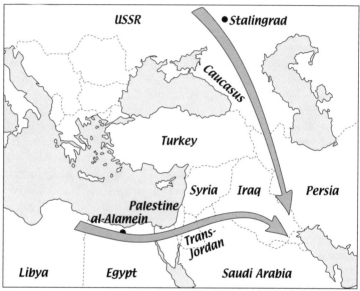

Map after Eppele after Kuhn. Updated for 1942 by E.-H. Schmidt.

designs for war against Great Britain. Supported by Admiral Raeder, they proposed an integrated strategy with the Mediterranean as center of gravity for 1940 and 1941. The Japanese raids into the Indian Ocean gave rise to the concept of a pincer movement overland from Libya and through the Caucasus into the Middle East, supported by a strong demonstration of Japanese fleets in the Indian Ocean. Given the actual state of the navy, some of these plans were mere fantasies. Paradoxically the service, which most actively promoted a 'Mediterranean Strategy' for the Reich, postponed stronger commitment because it could scarcely spare the ships. Thus the naval war predominantly remained an Italian affair.

THE LUFTWAFFE

In order to keep the Axis forces in Africa fighting, air superiority over the convoy routes was crucial. The same was true for moving large, motorized troop formations or supply columns through the desert. Lacking sufficient naval striking power, the Axis air forces in North Africa had four tasks: establish air superiority over the combat zone, provide ground support as 'flying artillery' of the panzer divisions, safeguard their own convoy routes, and strangle British supply lines.

In general the Luftwaffe was an effective medium-range strike force, designed and trained for close cooperation with ground forces in a European theater of war. It was never designed to carry out protracted strategic campaigns of its own against an enemy hinterland, and it lacked long range bombers and escort fighters for strategic air-to-sea warfare.[141] Despite excellent airmen there was a lack of trained staff officers who could design and execute long-term strategic missions. Without a consistent air strategy, improvisation became the guiding principle.[142] With the advent of Albert Kesselring as C-in-C of the 2nd Air Fleet, one of the few able strategists entered the stage. 'Smiling Albert' was an able diplomat, a vigorous leader in battle and, as such, an exception in Göring's Luftwaffe.[143]

Solid staff work was much needed. The vast distances covered by opposing armies in just a few days and the need to shift whole air corps around between Sicily, North Africa, and Crete, put heavy stress on ground staff. Air corps facilities had to be as mobile as the armies themselves if the army were not to outpace the range of its air cover, as happened to Rommel in 1942 or, worse, if ground services could not evacuate in time to avoid the enemy. Lack of mobility cost the Luftwaffe more than 400 grounded aircraft when the British pursued the retreating Rommel in 1941.

The Luftwaffe in the Mediterranean[144] never managed to wage a strategic campaign against the Royal Air Force. Unlike the RAF, it never systematically put pressure on the opponent's ground organization and his supply lines in the hinterland. When the Eighth Army flooded back from the battles of Gazala and Tobruk in June 1942, the Luftwaffe missed a golden opportunity to turn this retreat into a rout by attacking the densely packed columns along the coastal road.

By and large it carried out its assigned missions successfully. Despite usually being slightly inferior numerically, the fighters in particular enjoyed a technical superiority with their Me 109F until the arrival of larger numbers of Spitfires in 1942. Until then they could usually achieve local air superiority or at least deny it to the RAF. When the Luftwaffe concentrated a full air corps against Malta in the spring of 1942, it forced the RAF to the ground and gained full control of the skies after a four-week air offensive. But the Luftwaffe lacked the forces to be strong everywhere. Once the battle for Malta was handed back to the Italians, allowing the Luftwaffe to concentrate support in Africa for Rommel's attack against the Gazala line, it was only a matter of a few weeks before the RAF on Malta regained the initiative.

The British planes then harassed the convoy routes and attacked harbors, forcing the Regia Aeronautica to defend these bases instead of attacking Malta. And because they had to concentrate on Malta, the JU-87 and JU-88 Stukas could not prevent the Eighth Army from building up and digging into the fortified positions in front of Tobruk. Similarly, a potentially promising position like the island of Crete could never be fully exploited for concentrated and sustained air strikes against the Nile Delta, the Suez Canal, and the facilities of Haifa and Alexandria. There was only enough of the Luftwaffe for one focal point, and in summer 1942 there was just enough strength for one air offensive—against Malta—and the support of one ground offensive—the one which led to the fall of Tobruk.

Seeing the depletion of his air force, Kesselring was against any further advance into Egypt because he "considered it madness to attack an intact airbase."[145] The distance between one's air bases and the target defined the number of air strikes and their strength, and here the RAF had a clear advantage over al-Alamein. Having almost won the 'war for aerodromes,'[146] the Germans could not make use of all these favorable air bases because they lacked the necessary forces. The air battles over al-Alamein passed the initiative in the air firmly into the hands of the RAF and also the USAF, who made their first appearance here. There was no German field marshal before the invasion in 1944 who learned the lessons about enemy air superiority as hard as Rommel did in Africa.[147] The outcome of these battles was a clear indicator that the Luftwaffe had overreached its means on too many fronts. Al-Alamein thus foreshadowed the general decline of the German air forces.

THE PANZER AFRICA ARMY

What the Afrika Corps could achieve depended very much on given conditions over which, on its own, it had limited influence. It was part of the most effective fighting force of its time that, even under adverse circumstances and with numerical inferiority, could beat every opponent on the battlefield. Given appropriate conditions, the Wehrmacht retained this winning capacity until early 1945.[148] But the army as a whole was only partially motorized and most of its infantry division had to rely on horse-drawn transport.[149] One can actually speak of two German armies consisting of two handfuls of fully mechanized panzer and infantry divisions on the one hand[150] and, on the other, the bulk of its infantry moving at the same pace as their predecessors under Napoleon. The German formations which Rommel brought with him were fully motorized, but even he could not escape the 'two-army syndrome' because the Italian divisions were 'walking men with guns' and still sadly undermotorized. Field Marshal Keitel[151] and, on one occasion, Hitler himself asked the Italians not to send any additional trucks and tanks to Russia but to equip their divisions in Africa instead.[152]

Rommel's main striking force was the two panzer divisions. They brought with them the "practice of mechanized warfare, the doctrine of a total cooperation between all arms, and an intensively practised battle drill."[153] Even lacking technical superiority or numbers, this training gave them the edge over their opponents until al-Alamein.[154] Defeat came not because they were beaten in battle or their morale failed. The retreat from Tobruk in 1941 happened only because they could not replace their losses fast enough. They needed only four dozen new tanks to bring them back to the offensive. Montgomery never dared challenge the panzers in their own realm, even after his men had also received intensive training. Instead, having the resources to do so, he designed his battle carefully so that he would not have to fight the panzers in open ground.[155] From beginning to end it was the availability of resources that extended or limited the capacities of tanks, guns, and men on the battlefield. With ample replacements at hand, the Panzer Africa Army need fear no enemy, and even the occasional folly of its impulsive commander could be absorbed without failure. Without that backup it was lost.

Al-Alamein and its Place in History

It is a commonplace feature in many books and articles to label the Battle of al-Alamein one of the decisive battles of the Second World War. This assertion deserves closer scrutiny, at least when it comes to the German view of the North African theater. Certainly al-Alamein was the climactic battle of the North Africa Campaign. But as this paper contends, the land campaign was closely interrelated with the whole Mediterranean theater of operations and therefore cannot be separated from the war in Europe as a whole.

Thus the approach to the question of this battle's place in history has to be more finely analysed. It certainly cannot be reduced to investigating the fight between the Panzer Africa Army and the Eighth Army as an isolated event. For a full analysis and a comprehensive picture, three connected questions have to be answered. First, did the war in the Mediterranean have any decisive influence on the final outcome of the Second World War? Second, did the North Africa Campaign decide the war in the Mediterranean theater of operations? And finally, did the result of the Battle of al-Alamein make the difference between victory and defeat on that front? The sequence of these questions increasingly narrows the focus and thus helps identify the place in history of al-Alamein. Controversy remains, however, and for the sake of the practice of history this campaign will, hopefully, continue to be discussed.

WINNING THE WAR THROUGH THE MEDITERRANEAN?

Most contemporary German historians today agree that a German victory in the Mediterranean would not have affected the overall outcome of the Second World War, i.e., that the war could not have been won or lost between Gibraltar and the Suez Canal.[156] As long as the British line of communication across the North Atlantic remained intact, Great Britain would have survived the temporary loss of its imperial position in the Mediterranean. British strategy clearly reflected this perception. Throughout the war, maintaining the lifeline to the strategic, economic, and political hinterland of the United States remained as much Britain's top priority as severing the line continued as top priority for the Kriegsmarine.[157]

With a hostile Italy barring the central Mediterranean, its importance for commercial sea traffic was already virtually nil. The British Isles received most of their oil from the USA, not the Middle East.[158] The refineries in the Middle East were mostly employed for local supply, and it was more important to deny their use to the Axis, for whom oil supplies were the major logistical headache.

Any plans for a pincer move of Japanese forces from the East and of German–Italian armies through the Middle East towards India belong to the realm of speculation. With the USA and a costly land war in China on their back, Japan could not have sustained such an effort and, as long as Russia was not beaten, Germany could not spare the necessary divisions.

Nevertheless a Mediterranean Sea under full Axis control could have extended the war for a considerable period of time. It would have provided a political, strategic, and economic power base[159] and secured the southern flank against any attack. It would thus have added to the strategic depth of a German-dominated Europe, probably drawing countries like Spain, Vichy France, or Turkey much closer to the Reich. However, one should also take into consideration that, during the war in the Mediterranean, about 620,000 Axis soldiers[160] were lost together with hundreds of tanks and planes and hundreds of thousands of civilian and military shipping tonnage. German strategists, including Adolf Hitler, expected correctly that the initiative would pass to the Allies somewhere in 1943. The only chance for the Reich was then a war of attrition and exhaustion in which only unbearable costs could have convinced the Allies of the futility of continuing the war. In such a war every man and tank, every well-established position, would have counted.[161] Not ultimate victory but at the very least some good opportunities were squandered in the Mediterranean basin.

VICTORY IN THE MEDITERRANEAN?

As pointed out before, there were opportunities for the Axis to drive Great Britain out of the Mediterranean Sea and its littorals. The best chance of defeating an enemy comes when it is weak or staggering from a heavy blow. There were two clear opportunities for that.[162]

The first of these came when the loss of France coincided with the entry of Italy into the war, i.e., when Britain had suffered crippling losses, faced a German air offensive, and been threatened by an invasion of the mainland itself. At the same time, Italy held a couple of key positions in the Mediterranean, from which it could attack some of the most important British bases. They were mostly insufficiently guarded and could not have withstood a determined attack. In those cases where Italian forces could not dislodge their opponents, Germany could have helped out. After the armistice in France most of Germany's ground forces were unemployed and—what Hitler knew, but Churchill did not—there never was the intention of seriously launching Operation Sealion.[163] A temporary shift of the center of gravity to the Mediterranean through autumn and winter 1940 and 1941 would have secured Axis control of their southern flank.

The second opportunity was offered by the coincidence of favorable events in spring and early summer 1941. Rommel's lightning advance towards Egypt, the Germans' drive through the Balkans, and their occupation of Crete had turned the geostrategic situation in the eastern Mediterranean upside down. Added to this, heavy losses had seriously undermined Britain's capacity to contain a further advance of the Axis into the Middle East, where Vichy Syria and turmoil in Iraq created additional potential threats. Neither Churchill in London nor Cunningham or Wavell in North Africa had any illusions about the outcome if indeed the Germans meant business.

What they could only guess but could not know for sure in 1941 became obvious in 1942. The bulk of Germany's fighting power was firmly committed in Russia, and this campaign was eating up German resources faster than they could be replaced. But now the United States had entered the war with their industrial-economic output already reaching the battlefields and their military not far behind. Had Rommel reached the Nile Delta or even the Suez Canal, the impact would have been far less tragic than a year before when the loss of Egypt had left the British forces without a place to go in the region. Meanwhile the hinterland was now firmly controlled by Allied forces, and the infrastructure and lines of communication for continuing the war in the Middle East had been established. Against them was an Axis with no additional forces at hand to exploit a success. A standoff was by now the most a German breakthrough to Alexandria could have achieved.

DECISION IN THE DESERT

What, then, did the Battle of al-Alamein decide? Definition must begin in 1942 with the series of encounters that occurred in the four months between 30 June when Rommel reached the position and 2 November when he ordered the retreat he had hoped to label the decisive Battle of al-Alamein. The first of these was Rommel's initial attempts to break through 1–3 July, often called the 'Battle of Ruweisat Ridge.' Then came the series of thrusts and counterthrusts through most of July. Next was Rommel's last attempt to regain the initiative, called the Battle of Alam al-Halfa, 31 August to 2 September. Finally Montgomery's attack, begun on 23 October, forced the Panzer Africa Army out of its trenches by 1 November.

Seen from the German side, the month of July had already settled the issue. When the exhausted spearheads of the Panzer Africa Army could neither turn the pursuit of the Eighth Army into a rout and drive on through to Alexandria, nor dislodge the reinforced British troops from their fortified boxes, it became clear even to contemporary observers that this round was lost.[164] In view of the supply situation, many German strategists acknowledged that winning the North Africa Campaign was now out of the question. The best that could be achieved was to maintain a mobile defense keeping the Allies away from European soil as long as possible.[165]

In the first days of July Rommel still had a fair chance of keeping the upper hand,[166] but he could never expect to win an extended race for the buildup of forces, and he was as aware of this[167] as everyone else. His drive into the Battle of Alam al-Halfa bears many features of a desperate last attempt.[168] Montgomery during these days remained confident and never felt the situation getting out of hand.[169] A few German analysts still claim that the battle could have been won under certain circumstances, among them more fuel and ongoing incompetence of British leadership in battle[170] which had not even inflicted enough losses on the enemy to forestall his offensive. Some now proposed a retreat from al-Alamein to the Halfaya–Sollum area.[171]

Because the al-Alamein line could not be outflanked, it offered some advantages, and since retreat did not exist in Hitler's vocabulary, Rommel remained in position and awaited the inevitable. His only hope was that, as so often before, he could draw the

Eighth Army into a battle of his own design and inflict enough losses to kick the enemy off balance and wear down his offensive power. Then he could conduct an orderly retreat and start the game anew. He did, indeed, inflict heavy losses on the enemy, and Montgomery grew anxious about the unfavorable ratio between casualties and success. However, he was aware through 'Ultra' of the dire straits Rommel was in. He could, therefore, continue the battle of attrition in the certain knowledge that the Panzer Africa Army would reach breaking point sooner or later.[172]

Although not everybody in the OKW realized that al-Alamein marked the beginning of the end of the German presence in North Africa—that this time there would be no triumphant return of the Desert Fox—Montgomery sensed it. The desert war had become a series of battles of supplies which bravery and stratagems alone could never win.[173] Nevertheless, despite the heavy losses in the aftermath of 'Supercharge,' could Rommel—aided by Montgomery's own cautious pursuit—have saved enough men to revive his panzer army for further resistance?

For the German side the first battle was the final turning point: after July 1942 the Panzer Africa Army could not win a decisive victory. For one German participant it was, in retrospect, "the turning point of the desert war, and the first of the long series of defeats on every front, which foreshadowed the collapse of Germany."[174] Ultimate British victory was secured in the last al-Alamein encounter. It became clear then that Rommel would never again knock at the gates of Egypt.

However the Axis position in North Africa became untenable not only because of al-Alamein, but also because of the landing of American forces thousands of kilometers away in northwest Africa. Entering the theater through its back door, they opened a second front, ensuring that only by a miracle could the Germans win the 'Race for Tunis' and build up enough strength to maintain a bridgehead in the former French colony.

Threatened from two sides by superior armies, the German–Italian forces in North Africa were doomed. It would have been better to evacuate them for the defense of Italy. When the remnants finally surrendered in Tunisia, two great armies with another quarter of a million men were lost.[175] With the loss of Tunis, the Mediterranean Sea became hostile waters for the

Axis.[176] The importance of al-Alamein was then clear for anyone with eyes to see. Together with the disaster of Stalingrad in the fall of 1942, these twin events were indicators that the Third Reich had overstretched itself: its days of expansion were over.

NOTES

[1] Code name of Montgomery's final assault to break through the German positions on 3 November 1942.

[2] This also focuses the bibliography. Since the general course of events can be taken from a vast amount of readily accessible works from multi-volume official histories, to the numerous biographies of the participants, to comprehensive articles in collective works, no reference will be made to such sources. Notes will mainly refer to opinions, direct citations, and/or highly specialized accounts.

[3] There is a vast literature about the issue. The outstanding treatment so far is the study of Ralf-Georg Reuth, *Entscheidung im Mittelmeer*, Koblenz, 1985.

[4] Heinz Magenheimer, *Die Militärstrategie Deutschlands 1940–1945*, München, 1997, p. 22. Until his very last days in 1945 he insisted that England waged this war against its own better interests, and that it never should have come into it. Magenheimer holds Churchill responsible.

[5] Walter Baum & Eberhard Weichold, *Der Krieg der Achsenmächte im Mittelmeerraum*, Göttingen ,1973, p. 14; J.F.C. Fuller, *The Second World War*, New York, 1993, p. 90; Michael Howard, *The Mediterranean Strategy in the Second World War*, London, 1993, p. 4.

[6] Kenneth Macksey, *Albert Kesselring*, London, 1978, p. 104.

[7] Libya, a couple of Aegean islands around Rhodes, and Abyssinia and Somalia in East Africa.

[8] Albert Kesselring, "Krieg im Mittelmeerraum," Gerhard Stalling Verlag (ed.), *Bilanz des zweiten Weltkrieges*, Oldenburg, 1953, pp. 65–80, here p. 69; John Keegan, *The Second World War,* New York, 1990, p. 321.

[9] Gerhard Schreiber, Bernd Stegemann & Detlef Vogel, *Das deutsche Reich und der zweite Weltkrieg*, vol. 3, Stuttgart, 1984, (quoted: DR 3), p. 74.

[10] i.e., the 1939 German–Soviet demarcation line through Poland, the distance measured from Best Litovsk.

[11] Franz Halder, *Kriegstagebuch*, 3 vols., Stuttgart, 1962, entries 8.10.1940, 10.10.1940. While the material was shipped, the men were airlifted.

[12] Walter K. Nehring, *Die Geschichte der deutschen Panzerwaffe 1916–45*, Stuttgart, 1974, p. 189.

[13] Maxim of Confederate cavalry general Nathaniel Bedford Forrest (1821–77).

[14] As part of the Ottoman army, especially in Palestine.

[15] James Lucas, *Panzer Army Africa*, Abingdon, 1977, p. 22; Rolf Valentin, *Ärzte im Wüstenkrieg*, Koblenz, 1984, p. 33.

[16] Barrie Pitt, *The Crucible of War*, 3 vols, London, 1986, here Pitt II, p. 304.

[17] Cf. the definitive study of Rolf Valentin, *Ärzte im Wüstenkrieg*, Koblenz, 1984, on the German medical corps of the Panzer Africa Army; also Wolf Heckmann, *Rommels Krieg in Afrika*, Bindlach, 1981, p. 442.

[18] Reinhard Stumpf, "Probleme der Logistik im Afrikafeldzug 1941–1943," in: *Vorträge zur Militärgeschichte*, vol 7: *Die Bedeutung der Logistik für die militärische Führung von der Antike bis in die neueste Zeit*, Bonn, 1986, p. 214.

[19] Cf. Martin Wilmington, *The Middle East Supply Center*, London, 1971.

[20] German navy.

[21] Code name for the third, and finally successful, attempt to lift the Siege of Tobruk.

[22] When Rommel arrived in North Africa and launched his first offensive, he was a divisional commander.

[23] Lieut. General Sir Alan Cunningham, brother of Admiral Andrew Cunningham.

[24] Fuller, *Second World War*, p. 160.

[25] S.W.C. Pack, *Cunningham, The Commander*, London, 1974, pp. 197ff.

[26] For the role of deciphering intelligence operations in the Mediterranean cf. Ronald Lewin, *Entschied Ultra den Krieg?*, Koblenz, 1981; Alberto Santoni, *Ultra siegt im Mittelmeer*, Koblenz, 1985; Janusz Piekalkiewicz, *Rommel und die Geheimdienste in Nordafrika 1941–1943*, Munich/Berlin, 1984.

[27] Code name of the enciphering system and machine, variations of which were used in a couple of countries throughout the war.

[28] Lewin, *Ultra*, p. 208; Santoni, *Ultra siegt*, pp. 64f.

[29] Piekalkiewicz, *Geheimdienste*, pp. 172–79; Lewin, *Ultra*, p. 320.

[30] Basil Liddell Hart, *The Other Side of the Hill*, p. 246.

[31] Piekalkiewicz, *Geheimdienste*, p. 106.

[32] Lewin, *Ultra*, pp. 207, 229; Piekalkiewicz, *Geheimdienste,* p. 107.

[33] Piekalkiewicz, *Geheimdienste*, p. 186.

[34] Gerhard Schreiber, "Italiens Teilnahme am Krieg gegen die Sowjetunion," in Jürgen Förster, *Stalingrad,* München/Zürich, 1992, pp. 250–92, here pp. 251f; Werner Schütt, "Der Stahlpakt und Italiens Nonbelligeranza," in *Wehrwissenschaftliche Rundschau,* vol. 8, 1958, p. 500; *Josef Goebbels, Tagebücher 1924–1945,* 5 vols., (ed. Ralf-Georg Reuth), Munich, 1999, entries 31.1.1941, 29.4.14; The *Ciano Diaries,* (ed. Hugh Gibson), New York, 1946, is full of references to the anti-German sentiments of his country.

[35] Schütt, "Der Stahlpakt," pp. 498–521, here 502; again Ciano has numerous entries displaying the Duce's mixed and wavering emotions towards his son-in-law and foreign minister, Galeazzo Ciano: *The Ciano Diaries* (ed. Hugh Gibson), New York, 1946.

[36] Italian air force, Jack Greene & Alessandro Massignani, *The Naval War in the Mediterranean*, London, 1998, pp. 32–38.

[37] Karl Gundelach, *Die deutsche Luftwaffe im Mittelmeer, 1940–1945*, 2 parts, Frankfurt/Bern/Cirencester,1981, pp. 32f with some figures.

[38] The Italian navy.

[39] Halder, *Tagebuch*, entry 4.11.40.

[40] Greene and Massignani, *Naval War,* pp. 38–48.

[41] They sent twice the tonnage to the ground as the Italians.

[42] They bought some JU-87 from Germany.

[43] Greene and Massignani, *Naval War,* p. 77.

[44] Gerhard Weinberg, *A World at Arms*, Cambridge, 1994, p. 210.

[45] Ciano, *Diary*, entry 25.6.40.

[46] Italian C-in-C in North Africa. After the putsch against Mussolini he became minister of war of the fascist republic.

[47] For some revealing figures cf. Ray Moseley, *Zwischen Hitler und Mussolini*, Berlin, 1998, p. 149.

[48] F.W. v. Mellenthin, *Panzer Battles*, London, 1977, pp. 178f; Albert Kesselring, *The Memoirs of Field-Marshal Albert Kesselring*, London, 1953, pp. 105, 108; Heinz W. Schmidt, *With Rommel in the Desert*, London, 1973, pp. 490f.

[49] Baum and Weichold, p. 26. Mussolini himself was more than doubtful about the military qualities of his Italians, cf. Ciano, *Diary,* entries 29.1.1940, 21.6.1940.

[50] Enno v. Rintelen, "Mussolini, Parallelkrieg im Jahre 1940," in *Wehrwissenschaftliche Rundschau*, vol. 12, 1960, pp. 16–38, here pp. 18f; Greene & Massignani, *Naval War,* p. 31.

[51] Ibid, Rintelen, p. 16.

[52] Moselcy, p. 135.

[53] Lothar Gruchmann, "Die 'verpassten strategischen Chancen' der Achsenmächte im Mittelmeer 1940–41," in *Vierteljahreshefte für Zeitgeschichte,* vol. 18, 1970, pp. 456–75, here pp. 459f. Count Galeazzo Ciano was Mussolini's son-in-law and Italian foreign minister from 1936–February 1943. Ciano, *Diary,* entry 27.7.39, 6.8.39, and a couple of other entries in August 1939.

[54] It was signed on 22 May 1939. It was an offensive pact, but with an obligation for both partners to consult the other before any major action. The text can be found in Günther Schönnbrunn, *Weltkriege und Revolutionen 1914–1945 (Geschichte in Quellen,* vol. 5), München, 1961, p. 432; see also Schütt, p. 498.

[55] Schütt, "Der Stahlpakt," p. 516; Rintelen, p. 21.

[56] *Ciano's Diary,* entry 6.8.40.

[57] R.A.C. Parker, *Europa im zwanzigsten Jahrhundert,* vol.1 (Fischer, *Weltgeschichte,* vol. 34), Augsburg, 1998, p. 254; Gruchmann, pp. 459f.

[58] Rintelen, p. 19; Gruchmann, p. 457.

[59] Gruchmann, p. 459f; Andreas Hillgruber, *Hitlers Strategie,* 2nd ed., Munchen, 1982, p. 281; Rintelen, p. 17.

[60] Rintelen, p. 28. The originally planned attack against Yugoslavia had been banned by Hitler. The complicated politics in the Balkans between 1939 and 1941 are extensively discussed in Hillgruber's book and in Philipp Fabry, *Der Hitler-Stalin-Pakt 1939–1941,* Darmstadt, 1962.

[61] Rintelen p. 37.

[62] Hillgruber pp. 281, 292; Goebbels, Tagebuch entries 11.6.1941, 20.7.1941.

[63] Ciano, *Diary,* entry 29.10.1939; Schreiber p. 282.

[64] Ciano, *Diary,* entry 17.5.40; Schreiber p. 280.

[65] For an overview of the Italian involvement in the Russian Campaign, cf. the article of Schreiber.

[66] Winston Churchill, *The Second World War,* 2nd ed., London, 1954; here: Churchill vol. I, p. 370; Kesselring/Bilanz, p. 68.

[67] Pack, p. 212.

[68] Churchill vol. II, pp. 390f, vol. III, pp. 50f; Gundelach I, p. 26; Pack, p. 88f.

[69] Weinberg, p. 218; Schreiber *et al., Das deutsche Reich* 3, p. 598.

[70] Joachim Laude, "Die Eroberung Nordafrikas durch Montgomery," *Wehrwissenschaftliche Rundschau,* vol. 15, 1965, pp. 697–712, here p. 702.

[71] Arthur Bryant, *Triumph in the West,* London, 1959, p. 33.

[72] Howard, p. 4.

[73] Baum/Weichold, pp. 26–32, 125.

[74] Pack, p. 124; Williamson Murray, *The Luftwaffe 1933–1945*, Washington/London, 1996, p. 126.

[75] Ibid, p. 177.

[76] Pitt II, p. 335.

[77] For a comprehensive comparative assessment cf. Greene & Massignani, *Naval War*, pp. 32–38.

[78] Pitt III, p. 90.

[79] Pitt I, p. 286.

[80] Churchill III, pp. 16, 304; Fuller, *Second World War*, p. 156; Basil Liddell Hart, *Der zweite Weltkrieg*, 6th ed., Wiesbaden, 1985, p. 345; Kenneth Macksey, *Military Errors of World War Two*, London, 1987, pp. 93–97. For a comparative assessment of Allied and German tanks see Piekalkiewicz, *Panzerkrieg*, p. 160.

[81] A detailed example can be found in Schmidt, p. 125f, who led a German AT company in North Africa.

[82] Liddell Hart, *Der zweite Weltkrieg*, pp. 228, 341; Janusz Piekalkiewicz, *Der Krieg der Panzer 1939–1945*, re. Augsburg, 1999, p. 16; Macksey, *Errors*, p. 82; DR 4, p. 634; Montgomery, *Memoirs*, p. 104.

[83] Thomas L. Jentz, *Tank Combat in North Africa*, Atglen, 1998, p. 186f.

[84] The battle which preceded the Fall of Tobruk in 1942.

[85] In the Battle of Arras, 22–24 May 1940; cf. Piekalkiewicz, *Panzer*, pp. 74, 109.

[86] Jentz, p. 60.

[87] Macksey, *Errors*, pp. 79ff, 93–97.

[88] Howard, p. 23; Pitt I, p. 12ff.

[89] For which the British light tank formations earned the highest respect of their opposite numbers: Pitt II, p. 185.

[90] Fuller, p. 165; Nehring, p. 187; Howard, p. 23; Macksey, *Errors*, p. 100f.

[91] Liddell Hart, *Der zweite Weltkrieg*, p. 370.

[92] Pitt II, pp. 5f, 304.

[93] Liddell Hart, *Der zweite Weltkrieg*, p. 371; Bernard L. Montgomery, *El-Alamein to River Sangro, Normandy to the Baltic*, London, 1973, p. 17; Bernard L. Montgomery, *The Memoirs of Field Marshal Montgomery*, 3rd ed., London, 1958, pp. 112f, 199; Stephen Brooks (ed.), *Montgomery and the Eighth Army*, London, 1991, pp. 55–61.

[94] Macksey, *Errors*, p. 107; Pitt III, pp. 11, 90. For Montgomery's own ideas see note 26.

[95] For the Spanish position towards participation cf. Donald S. Detwiler, "Spain and the Axis during World War II," in *Review of Politics*, vol. 33, 1971, pp. 36–53. For the difficult situation of Vichy between Britain and Germany the very recent article Elmar Krautkrämer, "Gentlemens's Agreement zwischen London und Vichy," in *Vierteljahreshefte für Zeitgeschichte* 3/1998, p. 429–54.

[96] Hitler's ideas concerning possible options in the Mediterranean are reflected in his Directive no. 18 of 12 November 1940, cf. Walter Hubatsch, *Hitlers Weisungen für die Kriegführung 1939–1945,* 2nd ed., Koblenz, 1983, pp. 67–71.

[97] *Oberkommando des Heeres* = Supreme Army Command (Krautkrämer, "Gentlemen's Agreement," p. 429—i.e., the ground forces).

[98] Ralf-Georg Reuth, *Entscheidung im Mittelmeer*, Koblenz, 1985, pp. 18–24; Gruchmann, p. 465ff.

[99] See above note 4, Magenheimer, p. 23.

[100] H. v. Buttlar, "Gedanken über die italienisch-deutsche Kriegführung im mittleren Mittelmeer 1940/42," in *Wehrwissenschaftliche Rundschau,* vol. 1, 1951, pp. 38–46, here p. 39.

[101] Hillgruber, p. 82.

[102] Churchill to Ismay, 21.9.40, cf. Churchill vol. II, p. 417ff.

[103] He obviously perceived the situation around England with much less pessimism than he displayed in his speeches; cf. Hillgruber, p. 79f.

[104] Who later served with Rommel and was captured at al-Alamein.

[105] Halder, *Tagebuch*, entry 2.11.1940.

[106] Baum/Weichold, p. 113ff; DR 3, pp. 197, 209; Gruchmann, p. 472; Fuller, p. 91; Liddell Hart, *The Other Side of the Hill*, p. 234; Magenheimer, p. 74.

[107] Outlined in his Directive no. 32, "Preparations for the Period after Barbarossa," 16.9.1941; cf. Hubatsch, pp. 129–34; a couple of September entries in Halder, *Tagebuch*, are dealing with these considerations as well.

[108] The German word is *Auftragstaktik*; it is perceived as one of the secrets of German military success in the wars of the 19th and 20th centuries. Cf. Dirk Oettling, *Auftragstaktik: Geschichte und Gegenwart einer Führungskonzeption,* Frankfurt/Bonn, 1993.

[109] Weinberg, p. 349.

[110] Bodo Scheurig, Alfred Jodl, *Gehorsam und Verhängnis*, Frankfurt, 1991, p. 156.

[111] Laude, p. 700f.

[112] Kurt Maser, *Adolf Hitler: So führte und regierte er*, Koblenz, 1997, pp. 9, 33, 36.

[113] Hermann Balck, *Ordnung im Chaos: Erinnerungen 1893–1948*, Osnabrück, 1981, p. 471; the author served as one of the most successful German panzer generals in the East.

[114] Maser, pp. 19f, 75, 82.

[115] Kesselring's title "OB Süd"/C-in-C South is misleading. During the North Africa Campaign he was commander of the Luftwaffe only.

[116] Kenneth Macksey, *From Triumph to Disaster*, London, 1996, p. 130.

[117] Macksey, *Triumph*, p. 227.

[118] 'Our Sea,' the Italian slogan for its perception of what the Mediterranean should become.

[119] For the German political involvement in the Middle East and North African affairs throughout the war cf. Bernd Philip Schröder, *Deutschland und der Mittlere Osten im zweiten Weltkrieg*, Göttingen, 1975.

[120] Nine ships—cruisers and destroyers—sunk, seventeen damaged.

[121] Churchill vol. III, p. 687; Gundelach, p. 251.

[122] Hillgruber, p. 423; Fuller, p. 110ff.

[123] Churchill vol. III, p. 236.

[124] The 7th Air Division (i.e., the paras) had lost about half their strength, and altogether the invasion force had suffered higher losses than two German armies during the whole Balkan campaign.

[125] For Hitler the main reason for the invasion was the denial of the island as a jump-off point for air attacks against the oilfields in Romania.

[126] The German *Fallschirmjäger* wore green while the army was in field gray.

[127] Kurt Student, *Generaloberst Kurt Student und seine Fallschirmjäger*, ed. Hermann Götzel, Friedberg, 1980, pp. 198ff.

[128] Student, p. 349.

[129] A book title: Laddie Lucas, *The Thorn in Rommel's Side*, London, 1992.

[130] The two major works on supply in the North Africa Campaign are Martin van Creveld, *Supplying War*, Cambridge, 1997, pp. 188–217; but first and foremost Reinhard Stumpf, "Probleme der Logistik im Afrikafeldzug 1941–1943," in *Vorträge zur Militärgeschichte vol 7: Die Bedeutung der Logistik für die militärische Führung von der Antike bis in die neueste Zeit*, Bonn, 1986. For the debate about the importance of bottlenecks in road and sea transport and their implications for the conduct of the campaign, see the summary in Stumpf, p. 232ff.

[131] By the Long Range Desert Patrol and light reconnaissance motorized units.

[132] The Malta–Egypt controversy is part of every account of the campaign. A very detailed summary is Reuth, pp. 171–205; cf. also Walter Warlimont,

"Die Insel Malta in der Mittelmeer-Strategie des zweiten Weltkrieges," in *Wehrwissenschaftliche Rundschau,* vol. 8, 1958, pp. 421–436.

[133] Greene/Massignani, *Naval War,* pp. 225–31, and in their very detailed article "The Summer of 1942: The proposed Axis invasion of Malta," in *Command Magazine,* pp. 64–67, believe that it was possible. Joseph Attard, *The Battle of Malta,* Malta, 1994, p. 195ff, is convinced that it was not.

[134] Ernle Bradford, *Bastion im Mittelmeer,* München, 1986, p. 218, quoting a report of Governor Dobbie.

[135] Hillgruber, p. 37.

[136] Gruchmann, p. 456.

[137] C-in-C of the U-Boats, later C-in-C of the Kriegsmarine and, after Hitler's suicide, for a few days nominal head of state in 1945.

[138] Karl Dönitz, *Deutsche Strategie zur See im zweiten Weltkrieg,* 2nd ed., Frankfurt, 1972, p. 70f; Karl Dönitz, *Zehn Jahre und zwanzig Tage,* München, 1980, p. 155ff; Baum and Weichold, *Der Krieg,* p. 113ff.

[139] Kurt Assmann, "Die deutsche Seekriegsführung," in Gerhard Stalling Verlag (ed.), *Bilanz des Zweiten Weltkrieges,* Oldenburg, 1953, p. 115–32, here p. 126f.

[140] Mostly because of the resistance of Hermann Göring, second most powerful figure of the Third Reich and C-in-C of the Luftwaffe: "What's in the air is mine," cf. Dönitz, *Zehn Jahre,* pp. 127, 135; Assmann, *Bilanz,* p. 117.

[141] Kesselring, *Bilanz,* p. 152.

[142] Rohden, p. 32; Adolf Galland, "The Defeat of the Luftwaffe," in Eugene Emme (ed.) *The Impact of Air Power,* Princeton, 1959, pp. 245–60, here p. 250.

[143] The few able staff officers had often acquired their managerial skills in business or, like Kesselring, in civil service functions.

[144] The definitive account on the operations of the Luftwaffe in the Mediterranean is Karl Gundelach, *Die deutsche Luftwaffe im Mittelmeer,* 2 parts, Frankfurt, 1981.

[145] Kesselring, Memoirs, p. 123.

[146] Philip Guedalia, *Middle East 1940–1942: A Study in Air Power,* London, 1944, p. 163.

[147] Rommel barely survived the ground attack of an American fighter bomber in Normandy in 1944. Cf. his numerous reflections on air power in Basil Liddell Hart (ed.), *The Rommel Papers,* London, 1953, especially pp. 319–22.

[148] See for this idea and the underlying reasons Martin van Creveld, *Fighting Power: German Military Performance 1914–1945,* Washington,

1980, and also the introductory chapters in R.H.S. Stolfi, *Hitler's Panzers East,* Norman, 1991; Pitt II, p. 170.

[149] For details cf. Piekalkiewicz, *Panzer,* p. 15.

[150] Later called 'Panzer Grenadiers.'

[151] Chief of the Oberkommando der Wehrmacht (OKW), Hitler's Supreme Command of the German forces.

[152] Schreiber, pp. 263, 265.

[153] Pitt I, p. 247.

[154] Nehring, pp. 125, 188.

[155] Pitt II, p. 11.

[156] Hillgruber, p. 191f; Magenheimer, p. 153; Gruchmann, p. 475; Gundelach I, p. 40; Baum and Weichold, p. 105.

[157] Walter Warlimont, *Im Hauptquartier der deutschen Wehrmacht 1939 bis 1945*, 2 parts, Augsburg, 1990, here I, p. 240; Dönitz, *Deutsche Strategie,* p. 70f, quoting also a couple of British sources.

[158] Richard Overy, *Why the Allies Won*, New York/London, 1995, p. 44.

[159] Gundelach I, p. 40, quoting thoughts of Grand Admiral Erich Raeder.

[160] About 200,000 of them were Germans. The majority were captives, especially as a result of the capitulation in Tunisia.

[161] A that time nobody in Germany (or elsewhere) had an idea about the impact of a nuclear bomb. Had Germany not surrendered in spring 1945, Berlin instead of Hiroshima would have been the first target.

[162] Gruchmann, p. 472.

[163] German code name for a cross-channel invasion of Great Britain in late summer 1940. See Hillgruber, pp. 166–78 for a short account; K.Klee, *Das Unternehmen Seelöwe*, Göttingen, 1958, for a detailed account.

[164] Baum and Weichold, p. 237.

[165] Macksey, *Kesselring*, 132.

[166] DR 6, p. 655.

[167] Rommel Papers, pp. 254, 264–70.

[168] Baum and Weichold, p. 245.

[169] Cf. his diary notes in Brooks, p. 33; cf. Laude, p. 704.

[170] Among them some which are as authoritative as possibly biased: Nehring, p. 108. He lead DAK into this battle until he got wounded. Mellenthin—p. 175f.—was one of his staff officers. Cf. also Liddell Hart, *Weltkrieg*, p. 376.

[171] Pitt III, p. 86f; Kesselring, *Bilanz*, p. 73.

[172] Liddell Hart, *Weltkrieg*, p. 383; Piekalkiewicz, *Geheimdienste,* pp. 174–86; Lewin, p. 320ff.

[173] Walter Warlimont, "Die Entscheidung im Mittelmeer 1942," in Hans-Adolf Jacobsen and Jürgen Rohwer (ed.), *Entscheidungsschlachten des zweiten Weltkrieges,* Frankfurt, 1960, pp. 233–68, here p. 240; Montgomery, *El-Alamein,* p. 35; Brooks, pp. 34, 83.

[174] Mellenthin, p. 172.

[175] Eight German divisions with 130,000, six Italian with 120,000 and the air supply operation had almost annihilated what was left of the German air transport service after the heavy losses in Crete and Stalingrad.

[176] Kesselring, *Bilanz.*

Chronology of Events

12 March	A parade in Tripoli of the newly arrived units of the Afrika Corps.
24 March	The Afrika Corps attacks and captures al-Agheila.
31 March	The Germans strike at Marsa Brega.
3 April	Benghazi is captured by the Germans.
5 April	Addis Ababa, capital of Ethiopia, is captured from the Italians.
6 April	German forces invade Yugoslavia and Greece.
7 April	Derna falls to the Axis troops.
10 April	The British Army withdraws to Tobruk.
11 April	German panzer forces cut the Tobruk–al-Adem road. Two thousand British soldiers are taken prisoner, including three generals.
13 April	Tobruk is encircled and Bardia captured.
14 April	The German attacks on Tobruk are repulsed.
27 April	Part of the Afrika Corps thrusts across the Libyan–Egyptian frontier and captures Halfaya Pass.
28 April	Sollum falls to German troops.
1 May	Beginning of confrontation between Iraqi forces of the anti-British government of Rashid al-Ghailani.
15 May	General Wavell opens Operation Brevity, a limited campaign to gain jumping-off positions for a future and larger offensive.
16 May	The Duke of Aosta's forces surrender in Ethiopia. Rommel throws in a counterattack against the British.
20 May	German airborne invasion of Crete. The island is conquered by 1 June.
27 May	German panzer forces drive the British out of the Halfaya Pass.
30 May	The revolt in Iraq ends. Al-Ghailani goes into exile.
8 June	Commonwealth and Free French forces invade Syria.
15 June	Wavell's major offensive, Operation Battleaxe, opens.

22 June	The German Army invades Russia.
1 July	Wavell is replaced by General Sir Claude Auchinleck.
12 July	Vichy forces in Syria agree to an armistice.
17 November	British commandos raid what is believed to be Rommel's headquarters.
18 November	A new British offensive, Operation Crusader, opens.
19 November	Sidi Rezegh is captured by the Eighth Army.
20 November	Fighting continues around Sidi Rezegh.
21 November	The British garrison of Tobruk makes a sortie to link up with the forces in the Sidi Rezegh area.
22 November	The 21st Panzer Division attacks the British armor.
23 November	The German armor, now massed, defeats the piecemeal British tank attacks. New Zealand troops occupy Bardia.
24 November	Rommel flings a column over the Egyptian frontier.
26 November	General Cunningham, commanding the Eighth Army, is replaced by Ritchie. The British Tobruk force captures Duda and links up with the infantry force taking part in Operation Crusader.
29 November	Von Ravenstein is taken prisoner.
30 November	During the day severe German attacks are launched against the British corridor between Sidi Rezegh and Tobruk.
6 December	There is heavy fighting south of Sidi Rezegh, which lasts until 8 December.
13 December	Rommel's counterattack comes in and opens a five-day offensive battle.
17 December	The German effort fails and the German troops begin to withdraw from Gazala.
19 December	The Eighth Army recaptures Derna and Mechili.
23 December	Barce is recaptured by the British.
24 December	Benghazi falls to the Eighth Army.

1942

2 January	Bardia is recaptured.

5 January	The Eighth Army's attack opens on Halfaya Pass.
6 January	Rommel's offensive against the Eighth Army opens from a jump-off point at Agedabia.
8 January	The Eighth Army drives back Rommel from Agedabia.
12 January	The British take Sollum.
17 January	The Eighth Army recaptures Halfaya Pass.
21 January	Rommel's offensive reopens at al-Agheila.
23 January	The Afrika Corps recaptures Agedabia.
4 February	The Axis troops retake Derna.
14 February	After a two-week pause, Rommel renews his offensive.
30 March	German 2nd Air Corps launches a major air offense against Malta. The attacks continue until 28 April.
26 May	The third German offensive opens with an attack against the Gazala position.
2 June	The siege of Bir Hakim at the southern end of the Gazala position opens. Rommel begins to gap the British minefields. General Crüwell, commander of the Afrika Corps, is shot down and captured.
3 June	General Ritchie's counterattack fails. The British 150th Brigade is overrun.
10 June	The Free French holding Bir Hakim are ordered to withdraw.
12 June	The tank battle in the 'Knightsbridge' area opens.
13 June	The 'Knightsbridge' battle continues.
14 June	The Eighth Army begins a fighting withdrawal from Gazala.
16 June	The Axis troops attack at Sidi Rezegh.
17 June	The British Eighth Army withdraws to the Egyptian frontier.
18 June	The Afrika Corps opens its attacks upon Tobruk.
20 June	The German attack continues upon Tobruk.
21 June	Tobruk falls. Bardia is captured.
24 June	The Panzer Army advances into Egypt.

25 June	Auchinleck takes command of the Eighth Army.
27 June	The Germans battle for Marsa Matruh.
28 June	Marsa Matruh is captured.
1 July	The Panzer Army reaches al-Alamein.
2 July	The First Battle of al-Alamein begins.
3 July	Rommel breaks off the battle.
4 July	The Eighth Army's counterattacks go in along the Ruweisat Ridge.
10 July	The Australians capture the Tell Issa from the Italians.
26 July	The British attacks are held by the Germans and flung back.
13 August	Operation Pedestal succeeds, despite heavy losses, in shipping crucial supplies to Malta.
18 August	General Alexander to take over as Commander-in-Chief, Middle East. General Montgomery takes up his post as commander of the Eighth Army.
31 August	The Battle of Alam al-Halfa opens.
3 September	The New Zealand Division mounts a drive in the Alam al-Halfa sector to cut the German lines of communication.
7 September	The attack fails and Montgomery stops the battle: the Second Battle of al-Alamein.
1 October	A limited offensive is opened by the British in the Deir al-Munassib sector.
23 October	After an opening bombardment, the infantry corps of the Eighth Army goes into the attack. The armor of 10th Corps begins to move forward.
24 October	A reorganization and tidying up of the battle situation is put in hand in the area of 30th Corps. In 13th Corps sector the offensive makes little headway. The armor has still not gone forward.
25 October	Operations in the southern sector of the British line (13th Corps) are halted. The Germans launch panzer counterattacks. An attack by 10th Armored Division to capture the Wishka Ridge fails. Field Marshal Rommel returns to Africa from sick leave.

26 October   Air operations against the Panzer Army.

27 October   Torpedo-carrying aircraft from an RAF squadron attack and sink the tankers bringing fuel to the Panzer Army. The British attack 'Snipe' position. Montgomery produces a new plan, Operation Supercharge.

30 October   Australian attacks in the north of the line begin to 'crumble' the Germans.

2 November   The infantry goes in for Operation Supercharge.

3 November   The 9th Armored Brigade carries out its sacrificial attack.

3 November   The Battle of Aqaqir Ridge. The 1st Armored Division beats off the panzer counterthrust. In reply to Rommel's telegram on the need to withdraw from the al-Alamein positions, Hitler orders the Panzer Army to stand fast and fight. Rommel cancels the orders to withdraw.

4 November   Rommel orders the withdrawal to take place, as it is clear that the Eighth Army has outflanked him. General von Thoma, commanding Afrika Corps, is captured. The Panzer Army begins to withdraw from the al-Alamein battlefield.

8 November   Operation Torch opens. Allied troops land in French North Africa.

1943

12 May   The last organized resistance by Axis troops on the continent of Africa ceases.